'I Was Benny Hill's Toy Boy

A Life in Variety

By

Jon Jon Keefe

SMOKING GUN BOOKS

A SMOKING GUN BOOK

Published in Great Britain by Smoking Gun Books

2009

ISBN 09552661-3-0

All photos by Jon Jon Keefe except Front cover,125,126 by Ken Sedd,,
Pages 1,128,133 & 185 Thames TV

SMOKING GUN BOOKS LTD
1 Golfside Close London N20 0RD

'To Jo and my children,
The Sunshine in my life'

Index

1. I Was Benny Hill's Toy Boy

T hat's me standing next to Benny Hill, one of the world's most loved comedians. That's me dressed as an old woman, as a friar, a parking meter attendant, an Arab, a pilot and in an outlandish pink cowboy suit as the Gay Caballero. I was Benny Hill's toy boy. Now, don't jump to

conclusions: that merely means I was the youngest of Benny's permanent corps of characters. My professional name is Jon Jon Keefe. Benny said it must be very difficult going through life named after two toilets. I said doubly so as my sister's name is Lulu.

This journey through my life reads like a bad luck story, where I am always the bridesmaid and never the bride. As the years have gone by, that seems to have been my own overwhelming impression, of almost achieving my goals, but never quite. I started writing this story in my head many years ago and then it seemed to be true, a tale of 'poor me, what have I done to deserve not achieving my ambitions. I'm a good guy, why them and not me?' But upon writing this story, I find that instead of reading like a life unfulfilled, I am amazed and

1

happy at the richness of my experiences and the interesting diversity of the characters I have spent my life with. Far from feeling thwarted in my life's travel as I write, I am filled with the joy of the abundance that my life is now overflowing with.

2. Born in the War – a True Cockney

I am sixty-nine years young and, from as early as about two and a half to three years old, I have been made aware of the quality of my Englishness. 'Impossible!' I hear you say. 'No such staunch adult perceptions can be experienced by one so young.' To understand this proud feeling of being English, you need to have experienced the world I was thrust prematurely into, a world at war: 1939.

My family were ordinary, hardworking, lower class people. Both my parents were of Irish stock. My mother's lineage was one or two generations back; my father was born in Northern Ireland and left home to settle in London when he was only fourteen. I only learned this two days after his death when he was only forty-nine years of age. He was born illegitimately in a Catholic enclave of Belfast and was chastised and beaten by his mother for the shame he had brought her. So I grew up without realising that I was of Irish descent. I am so proud to have been born in St Bartholomew's Hospital: a Cockney. I fiercely defended not only my Englishness but the fact that I belonged to a very select group of stoic people within the English nation, therefore counting myself doubly special. I was born a true Cockney.

To be a genuine Cockney was not something afforded to a great number of people although many famous Londoners made claim to the fact. It was not enough to be born within the sound of Bow Bells, it was necessary to have the City of Westminster stamped on your birth certificate and that was only possible if you were in the catchment area around St Bartholomew's Hospital. Max Bygraves, Tommy Steele, Sir Maurice Micklewhite*[Michael Caine]*, all of these erstwhile Cockneys would have needed ears like Prince Charles to hear Bow Bells from the Elephant and Castle – south of the river.

So why did I feel so proud to be English at such an early age? I grew up listening to stories about what my family and their friends were putting up with as they were bombed and starved and sometimes killed. But we managed to turn horrific events into laughter – the true embodiment of the British spirit. We had huge admiration for great comedians like Benny Hill, who could also turn tears into laughter. All the great comics were able to make us laugh at our foibles and hardships and were much loved because they were so adept at it.

As a family we were bombed out of our house in Colombia Buildings, Hassard Street, Bethnal Green. I was born prematurely and spent my early months in a suitcase for a bed. My grandma said it was the easiest way to transport me when the bombs started dropping. We had a direct hit on the flats that we lived in and half the building was demolished. After that, my family spent time sleeping on the platform of the nearest Tube station until we were rehoused to the country, Dagenham in Essex. But even there we were bombed again. I thought Hitler must have had a personal grudge against my family..

The picture a child builds of his station in life is drawn by conversations he hears from his parents, aunts, uncles and extended members of his own family as well as neighbours and friends. My

4

influences must have been optimistic, noble and God-fearing, because all I can remember is a group of people putting up with the most awful deprivations and trials and still being optimistic, generous and positive. So my Englishness was moulded by people willing to give their lives for something they did not know much about, people who trusted those who led and governed them to make decisions for them that might cost them and their family their lives.

Music and laughter was always present wherever we called home.There was a camaraderie and a happiness that permeated every day. There was rationing but people shared. There were bombs dropping, destroying people's possessions and yet people shared. There was hurt and pain and suffering and people came together to help and share in others' grief. And through all this there was music and laughter, I remember the sounds of rooms full of people singing, "We'll meet again, don't know where, don't know when, but I know we'll meet again some sunny day." I remember Max Miller and Tommy Handley and a whole host of comedians trying to get us to look on the bright side singing "It's a long way to Tipperary".

As a child I learned of the heroic things members of my own family were doing. A mystery man called Uncle Johnny who had got himself into the Navy despite being too young, going on the missing list, blown up at sea and reappearing later in his uniform and going back again. I remember clearly the sound of a doodlebug. I remember having to stop everything and run to the Anderson shelter with my mother, brother, cousin Terry and Grandma and I remember the cold dank smell in the shelter in torch light. We cuddled up in a blanket and I was pressed in my Grandma's arms, so even though there were bombs falling and explosions, I still felt safe, warm and loved. I learned about red-hot shrapnel, what it was and where it came from. I learned about V2 rockets when one fell some way a way and broke all the windows in our house. I learned about the pleasure of Bovril and Ovaltine and my Grandma's bread and butter pudding. My Grandma's ability to turn ordinary not-too-fresh bread into a food of such delight was so great that no *cordon-bleu* chef has been able to match her since. It seems that deprivation brings out the best in people. I learned about trust, caring and sharing, compassion and understanding, happiness and love. There was no cynicism, no back-biting, no negative feeling of 'why me?' or 'why us?' Everyone was in the same boat. People were knocked down and they all helped each other to get up and go again. Each day was dealt with as it arose, not knowing what that day might bring. I remember waking up in a Morrison shelter (an indoor shelter of 3/8-inch thick metal plates of iron with wire mesh sides of six foot by four foot) in the front room. I learned about getting out of bed in the morning after an air-raid and sticking your foot out of the covers in the middle of winter in the freezing cold and getting your mum to warm your vest and pants by the oven in the kitchen before you got up into a freezing cold house with ice on the inside of the windows. I learned from very early on how to lay a fire and how to put a newspaper over the front of the fire to draw it up the chimney, I learned how to make tea and toast and I was trusted to do it without setting light to the house or burning or scalding myself. I learned very early on about self reliance and I learned about things that were expected of me. I learned about pulling my weight when my mother was on her own and had to look after us when father was away in the Army.

Add to this heavy mixture a serious bout of Catholicism and you can see the heavy burden I had to bear as a small child. I was expected to be God-fearing, honest and true. And I knew that if I stepped out of line, I was liable to be taken to task by not only parents but aunts, uncles, grandparents, school teachers, policemen; in fact anyone who was older and bigger than me – or so it seemed. I never cowered under this pressure. In fact, there was a security in knowing your place in life and from there endeavouring to rise to a more elevated position. I did not know how I was going to achieve this grand position from such a lowly position in the pecking order. It was enough just to be able to stay alive, to avoid being killed by falling bombs, and trusting that people bigger than you would be charitable enough to share what little food there was.

This was heady stuff indeed for a child to conjure with as a part of growing up in such troubled but happy times. It feels now looking back that nothing was taken for granted, chiefly because you didn't know how long you would be alive. But you were secure in the fact that you said your prayers and went to Mass and that meant that if and when you died, you would surely go to heaven because you and your family and country were in the right for what you were fighting for.

How could I not be ingrained as a God-fearing Englishman, when some of my earliest experiences were as heavy and full of such deep meaning?

So, with the sounds of '*Land of Hope and Glory*' ringing in my ears, at fifteen years of age I sallied forth into a world with not a certificate anywhere to prove I was as intelligent as I believed I was. I was a small boy, bright and a member of all the sports teams at school. I was particularly keen on football. I remember that the boots we wore to play football in were made out of the toughest heavy leather and the ball weighed a ton. When they both got wet, it was all you could do to lift your foot off the ground let alone do a Stanley Mathews dribble.

I was a very good swimmer and, as soon as I could swim my brother and I went to the local outdoor pool almost every day of the six-week summer holidays. We would be there from 10 a.m. until 5 p.m. , while my mother and father were at work. All day, every day we spent swimming, diving, playing in the open-air pool at Valence Park. We would be given some pocket money, a few Spam sandwiches and some sweets. Our greatest pleasure was found in a packet of Smith's crisps which came with a blue salt wrapper to spread on the crisps, and a cup of boiling Bovril clasped between fingers that were wrinkled and white from hours of being in the water. When my own children were about the same age as I was then, about eight, I tried to introduce them to the delights of Bovril as we finished a swimming session at the local multi-million pound municipal baths where I now live. I jokingly spouted off about how well off they had it now not like in my day, no facilities not a lot to eat as the Germans had bombed our chip shop our staple diet food centre. I proffered a steaming mug of Bovril, which I was amazed to find I was able to buy at such a modern emporium: they smelled it, gingerly tasted it and promptly spat it out in disgust! What had been a delicacy to my brother and I was dismissed as being not much better than cat's pee!

3. My Friend God

The more I questioned the relationship I had with God when I was young, the more I understood what a great sense of humour he has. As far as I can remember he was always there, tutting at my misdemeanours and opening his loving arms at my times of trial and tribulation. But He always left me to my own resources - and gave me my belief in our total freedom of choice.

As a small, frail, though tenacious lad, I was instilled with an unusually high degree of responsibility. I think this partly arose from my father's medical condition. I didn't know at the time what caused his incredible mood swings, but at the age of about seven, I found myself kneeling by the fireplace praying to my friend God, asking him to save my father from death, because otherwise I was going to find it difficult to look after my diminutive mother and my rapscallion five-year-old brother. Another time, I watched as my father was loaded into an ambulance and taken off to Rush Green Hospital, and prayed, 'Dear God, please make my father better. He is in so much pain and if he dies I don't know how I will be able to look after my Family.'

God must have listened to me because my father always came home again and I could get on with being a boy again. With ever increasing visits to my knees, asking God to help me, I became aware that I was accepting more and more responsibility for what was happening, and steeling myself for the day that my friend God might be too busy or too tied up with everybody else asking him for his help

10

and knowing that just not catching his attention this time would mean that I would have to take over the responsibility of looking after my family.

My father suffered horribly with duodenal ulcers. He was a tough man, with a fierce sense of duty and fair play. He was a hard taskmaster, had high ideals and fought ferociously for all things right and proper. But his family was the most important thing to him.

It was two days since my last prayers to God when I found out what was the underlying source of my father's brittle nagging pain. His ulcers were constantly being operated on and the scars on his abdomen were obvious to see. He weathered the intrusion of the surgeon's knife and as they cut more and more of his stomach away, I asked my friend God to save him again and if possible cure him so that I would not have to bother him again, as I was sure he had lots of other things to be getting on with. Though this was very important to me and my family, I thought we may not be on top of his list seeing as how he had already saved us from being bombed out twice. He must also be very busy sorting out the world's problems after the war.

My father got cancer of the oesophagus. He had even more difficulty eating than he had had with his ulcers. One day, whilst kneeling talking to my friend God, he was taken to the hospital again to have a piece taken out of his windpipe and a piece of synthetic material put in its place. I visited him in hospital and he was so determined to get better and come home.

He survived the operation and came home again to survive another two years in which his strength of character and Jack Russell spirit made him survive the hard fight and slog. He had always placed himself trustingly in the hands of his doctors as people did in those days, thinking that professionals who looked after your well-being doctors, teachers, policemen all knew what they were doing and knew what was best. I only ever heard my father question his treatment once, and that he thought they were experimenting on him with his new wind-pipe. I was in no position to agree or disagree as I watched him pour half a jar of Heinz baby food into his mouth and proceed to encourage it down his gullet with varying widths of flexible cane to enlarge his gullet to allow the food to reach his stomach. He never moaned, he just got on with it ever positive that he was going to get better. His life-long bad health gave him terrible mood swings, from smiling happy-go-lucky to hateful physical violence. But we would forgive him everything, seeing how hard he was clinging to life. He would come home from work upset at not being recognised for how well he thought he was doing his job and not being rewarded financially or moved up in the ranks. It was strange as a child not knowing what problems changed a house that was full of music and happiness one moment, into a place that felt alien and black as hell.

It was only two days after he died that my mother told me his deep down pain was of being born illegitimtely,when being a bastard was a really bad thing. If I had known this I am sure I could have helped him come to terms with this, but people didn't talk about such things then. I was so sad it was too late and he had died.

Ours was the most open house in the Banjo, *(our cul-de-sac was shaped like a banjo, hence the name)* and the door was always open. We had a Joanna *(piano)* and both my mother and father could play and the radio was always on. My friend God gave my brother and I a good musical ear and we were always singing.

My brother and I would go to the Saturday morning pictures to see 'Old Mother Riley, Laurel and Hardy, Bud Abbot and Lou Costello Will Hay, The Lone Ranger and Tonto'. Watching the bouncing ball on the screen and singing The Odeon song.

'We come along on Saturday morning greeting everybody with a smile, We come along on Saturday morning knowing its well worth while, As members of the Odeon Club we all intend to be good citizens when we grow up and champions of the free, We come along on Saturday morning greeting everybody with a smile, smile, smile, greeting everybody with a smile.'

That's where the true spirt of Englishness was born - Saturday morning pictures, 'Champions of the free' at nine years of age. I would enter the talent competitions. I would sing to an audience of a thousand screaming kids: *'I'll Take You Home Again Kathleen' 'See the Pyramids Along the Nile'*. I shared a seat with a nine-year-old beauty named Irene Dale and she would be proud to be with me. I don't know if she knew it but Irene Dale was my first crush. I would walk home with her to Nicholas Road, one of the toughest roads in the neighbourhood. If you were good at at football fighting or singing you were safe, although my brother got my head punched in a couple

13

of times telling some kids he would get his big brother on to them and me all of four stone in weight.

Dad did shift work at the *Ford Motor Company* in Dagenham. Mum was a dressmaker at Gardener's Corner in Aldgate in London. Mum would get us up and dressed ready for school then go off to work, and trying all the time not to wake Dad if he was on nights. His shift work became a major controlling influence in our lives. Six till two two till ten ten till seven. Dad was a very light sleeper and it didn't take much to wake him. The contrasting time zones my father's body was in on a rotating basis was far from ideal for someone who suffered with duodenal ulcers. Never one to shirk his paternal duties, he stuck to the task of looking after his family.

Although there was a school just one hundred yards from our front door, we could not go to it because we were Catholics. So that meant we had to trek to St Joseph's Roman Catholic school, three miles away, rain or shine, winter and summer, with instructions from either parent to look after my brother. My younger brother needed very little looking after and more times than not it was the other way around. We crossed major roads every day on the way to and from school, passing through enemy territory: Protestant schools. We were never told why we could not go to the school across the road with the other kids who lived in our street and why we were Catholics. We just accepted it.

We often arrived at school tired, wet, bedraggled and late. We were taught by Benedictine nuns; Mother Loyola was the Headmistress, quiet and resolute. Mother Vincent was a small nun with glasses and she looked and acted like a Japanese camp commandant in *The Bridge on the River Kwai*. Mother Bernadine was warm and comforting, and many years later I heard she became a lesbian. Mother Carmel was gruff with a mustache. The nuns could be both loving and ruthless. Our attention was brought to God's power of fire and brimstone, and we were taught that it was in our own best interests to be good if we hoped to enter the gates of Heaven, and not be cast down into the depths of Hell. I took this to heart and became a second division altar boy. There was a group of altar boys who lived near the church and they were the *crème de la crème*, the first team. They did the early morning masses and Benedictions. They were known as The Towlers, and they were really holy. I think one or two of them went on to be priests. The second divisioners were not half as holy; we were stand-ins and substitutes, but we tried our best.

What saved me and my brother was that we were great singers and we were in the choir. This was a feather in our caps and helped to save our souls. But my brother got us kicked out of the choir for messing about. We also got kicked out of the Cubs and the Scouts. We weren't great Catholics, but we were good-as-could-be Catholics, under the circumstances.

One day an incendiary case with three thousand fire bombs in it landed smack dab in the middle of the Banjo. The case split open and bombs spewed out and stuck in the roofs and gutters of the houses, but with God's good luck none of them went off. I can remember a fireman coming through the bedroom window and carrying me on his shoulder down the ladder. I wondered what I had done to upset the Germans as they seemed to come looking for me wherever I lived. All the neighbours and firemen thanked God for our good luck.

What I remember was different about people then was we thanked God for our good luck and sought his help and comfort when things went wrong. I remember seeing a Spitfire chasing a German plane so low that I could see the pilot firing his guns. We spent a lot of time playing in the street and we would find pieces of red hot metal that we found out was called *shrapnel.*

Being a Catholic seemed to put more pressure on me than it did the other kids in the Banjo, who were all Protestants. Hell loomed large in the nuns' explanation of God's plan for wayward boys and girls, so all my thoughts and actions were heavily mulled over, in relation to their quotient of sin factor. I think this tended to make me less spontaneous than I would have been had I been a Protestant. Tommy Stringer, Ronnie Loft and Georgie Lane were all more carefree than I was, and even my brother seemed to slant more to the call-yourself-a-Protestant-and-not-have-to-go-to-church-too-often brigade.

I know I had an old head on young shoulders now, but it was not obvious to me then. What with the turmoil in the house and the indoctrination by the nuns, I was really weighed down by the world. Being good was something to aim for and I worked hard at it. I became a mediator and a referee, rules for games had to be kept or what was the point of the game. It was irritating because the kids just wanted to get on with the game not caring about the rules. God and I were getting along just fine. I said my prayers and went to church. Then one day Tommy Stringer told us all about masturbating. He had learned how to do it from his older brother Charlie. As naive as we all were, we made a camp behind a wall and all began to rub. Compared to all the other trials and tribulations up until this point in my life, my relationship with God was about to take a very serious move, from venial, to mortal sin. Tommy Stringer was not the Devil, but surely the Devil had whispered in his ear to create torment and self doubt in this Catholic's life. So much confusion was created from such a natural act, the pleasure was immeasurable, but the recriminations after the act were cataclysmic.

I had hardly noticed there were girls living in the Banjo up to this point in my life. I had been too busy establishing my place in my peer group. I could hold my own in all sports and was above average at swimming, football, cricket, and all the street games: *British Bulldog, High Jimmy Knacker, Knock down Ginger, Tibby Cat.* But now the Devil's emissary Tommy Stringer had opened up a whole new way of thinking. My mother and father's best friends, Mr and Mrs Smith, lived next door and we spent a great deal of time in and out of each others' houses. Every Friday evening, regular as clockwork, both of our families would go to the Mayfair Cinema to watch Margaret Lockwood, Jean Kent and my own real favourites Patricia Roc and Jean Simmons. I had been watching them for years, but after Tommy Stringer's introduction to the sin club, their contours took on a whole new meaning. Friday evenings became much more thrilling. Mr and

Mrs Smith had a daughter called Doris and, prior to my introduction to the sin club, she had been given short shift when trying to join in our games. She had been treated like boys treat girls, until they notice the bumps on their chests. All of a sudden I would make sure I was sitting next to her when we went to the picture palace this was a term I used till I was grown up, and a brush against her knee would ensure that I would be distracted from what was happening on the silver screen. We would get home and I would press my ear against the wall, hoping to hear her getting undressed to go to bed. Then I would get into bed and the recriminations would start. Why did God allow these thoughts and actions happen to me. I was confused and repentant, the feelings of guilt were many times worse than the fleeting delight the pleasures gave me, and the recriminations would go on for hours and days, until the next time.

So it was then created, the never ending cycle of pleasure and guilt, guilt and pleasure. But I finally decided that it was a natural act and if God had not wanted me to do it then he would not have invented it in the first place. This deduction was completely overidden by the nuns teaching on original sin, just the thought and not the act, was enough to be a sin anyway. It didn't help that I sat in class next to a girl who took great delight in encouraging me to brush up against her leg whenever we could. Some lessons were a hot blur. Mother Vincent, our teacher, was a small fierce woman in her nun's head dress and long black gown. Some of her lessons were some of the most highly charged moments of my tormented life. We sat in double desks and there were forty-nine children in our class. The girl I sat next to was much bolder than me and I spent a great deal of the lesson with her hand in my lap. Feeling the effect and watching my flushed face just spurred her on. That year my grades took a nose dive. Questions were asked about my performance and I was hardly able to divulge what was going on, so I took on a more sullen attitude and became more introspective.

I was still praying to my friend God, but more dispassionately than before. Life was becoming much more confusing. Surely the Division One altar boys were not being subjected to this intrusion with their communication with God. They still did all the top Masses and celebrations and were some of the top scholars in the school. Their Godliness seemed to be paying off. God seemed to be rewarding them for their purity of thought. But I was in a constant state of confusion. I knew I wasn't bad: I always sprang to the defence of the underdog and fought against bullying and oppressive behaviour, but I was always having to say sorry for my impure thoughts and actions. This seemed to become more prevalent in my prayers, as I didn't want to be hypocritical. How could I keep asking God for his help in my family's tussle with survival, when I knew it would be almost impossible not to ask him for forgiveness after another one of those sessions. I was totally confused, and so I put my thought processes into neutral and the prospect of Limbo loomed large for what seemed like eternity.

It seemed at the time that it was only me who was going through

19

this terrible torment, pursuit of honesty, dependability, holiness. I must have seemed a very serious soul indeed for one so young. I cared about everything and doing everything properly. My priority was getting all things right first time and within the rules and regulations. I seemed to have the weight of the world on my shoulders. I hated the process of elimination and procrastination I put myself through before making any kind of decision.

Looking back, my brother did not seem to be straddled with the same earth-shattering decisions about anything, and had the capacity to be unruly and rapscallion in almost everything he did. He was a walking trouble factory and he and my father did not see eye to eye. He had a capacity for fun that I never had. His 'devil-may-care' attitude went down well with grown-ups, his attitude to most things seemed to be do what you want have a good time and if you get caught so be it. He was funny, spontaneous and a fun-loving rascal to boot. He wasn't being bad he was just being a boy while I was going on thirty.

All the confusion and upset of what would or would not happen to me and my family and God, made me lacking in self confidence. This became crashingly evident the night before sitting my 11-plus examination. I couldn't sleep, thinking of the importance of the next day's exams, and what failure might mean for my future. Would I have to spend the rest of my school days in underfunded Catholic schools, and have to leave school at fifteen and God-knows-what future? I prayed to God to help me sleep and give me the knowledge to pass the exams and promised I'd be good forever. Two, three, four, five o'clock came and went. I don't think I slept at all! By the time it was morning, I was totally drained. I pulled myself down the stairs in the cold. I lit the oven and put my vest in to warm it before I put it on. I ate some cereal, toast and milk, then I hauled my brother out of the door for the three mile hike to school for the exams that would determine if I would progress educationally or just become some more East End fodder

Even now, fifty years later, I can remember the feeling of exhaustion, being drained of energy and filled with the oppression of the task that lay before me. The exam would determine my whole future and I was in no mood for my brother's reticence to get to school at all. School and my brother did not see eye to eye. He did not give a damn about its claims of educating him for a great future. He figured his future was in his own hands and History, Geography and English certificates were of no value money-wise. He already had some jobs that were, by fair means or foul, getting him a good living wage for a grown-up man at the time and he was only ten. Working in the butcher's, working in the market, he was *Jack the Lad* and liked by everyone. The people he worked with had no qualifications, save for making bundles of ready cash. They relied upon themselves to look after themselves and were bold and confident enough to make their own way in the world and their security was up to them.

On the day of the 11-plus, I remember climbing the steps to the school, arriving just on time. I didn't have enough time to collect my thoughts before the exam. Assembly, hymns, prayers, including a last prayer for help to my God, in my hour of need, a quick soul search to see what state of holiness my soul was in and how good I had been of late, for God to warrant helping me through this day. My good to bad quotient seemed to come out where it always did: fair. I hoped the kind benevolent God that the nuns preached so often about, would be evident today.

The exams passed in a blur. I can remember nodding with tiredness over some of the papers. Things that I knew I knew, just disappeared from my brain. I was in turmoil. All reason left me as I yawned over the papers. What had I done that was so bad that God would desert me like this? Tired, unable to reason, drained of the ability to answer questions that I would stroll through if I had not been put under the pressure of being examined. The test was the ability to function under duress. All my insecurities ganging up on me. The Devil beckoning me, recriminations of days with a girl's hand in my lap, as Mother Vincent hammered home the basic needs of a good education.

Was sex so bad that it could mean the destruction of your whole future? Surely everybody else was going through the same patterns of thoughts, dreams and explorations. A quick look around the exam room at the Division One altar boys answered my question! With God's undivided attention, they were flying through all the questions with speed and precision, no hang-dog expressions, no fretting, no sighs. The questions when answered would secure their future, due to their attention to God's need for his children to supplicate themselves to him. They would be rewarded.

I knew I had not done well in my examinations. For those of us who had not passed, we were told that we could look forward to a menial, bleak future filled with very little chance of tasting the higher things in life. The kids who passed the 11-plus would go on to uniformed dress codes and the rest of us would be left to our own resources, or at best our parents' very meagre resources. We were told we could be assured of a life in menial circumstances, in factories and service jobs and, in some cases, a life of straight villainy.

I know a piece of me had been destroyed and I was to carry the stigma of my failure for the next fifty years. Being the Catholic that I was, I never blamed God for not being there in my hour of need, instead I did the good Catholic thing of blaming myself for my imperfections and sexual deviations.

The last six months at St Joseph's, I saw quite a division between those going on to Grammar school and those going on to Comprehensive school. The Comprehensives steeled themselves for a future of hardship and aggression and set upon a course of relaxation and indifference. We deduced that if we were going to be fodder, what was the point of working too hard. Even I became more relaxed and became quite adept at marbles and cigarette playing cards. We played marbles into the two cups of manhole covers and flicked cigarette cards up against the wall. I had a serious collection of marbles and cards.

One morning, I was awakened by my father asking me where my brother was, as he wasn't in his bed, or even in the house or garden. Through sleep-laden eyes I said I didn't know. There was a feeling of great menace hanging over the house and my nine-year-old brother was nowhere to be found. Nobody had a telephone so we were unable to call anyone for help. We searched the Banjo and the top street and he was nowhere to be found. My father was going mad at what my brother could have got up to, my mother and I didn't know what to make of the situation and especially at the consequences of what my Father might do to him when he found him. Then there was a loud rap on the door. Father opened it to be greeted by the local bobby. 'Sorry to disturb you so early Mr K., but are you missing one son who answers to the name of Patrick?'

'Yes,' said my father. 'Has something happened to him?'

'Well,' said the Bobby, 'it seems he made his own way to school this morning, rather earlier than usual – in fact about 5.30 a.m. – to meet a friend of his whom he had challenged to a marble tournament. He was doing rather well when we found him at about 7 a.m.'

On hearing this information, I ran upstairs to my prized cache of marbles hidden in a box under my bed. 'You git! You horrible little git!' Some of my best marbles were gone: my doublers and my candy stripes. How had he managed to get them out from under my bed without me waking up? This incident seemed to show how life would continue for both of us: me hanging onto things honestly gained and worked for and my brother on a course of getting what he wanted by fair means or foul.

My father marched me to the school to confront my brother in Mother Loyola's office. I gloated at the prospect of my brother's certain beating. True to form, he got another whacking and was hung on the back of the door. Needless to say, I hid my cigarette cards where nobody could find them but me. I know the small issues like this, of being punished by having my hard-won marbles confiscated, even though I had done nothing wrong, further entrenched the feeling of injustice that I have about the way perpetrators and victims are dealt with.

The last months of my primary school year were all about girls. They held an enormous amount of interest to me and I tried to learn as much as I could about the difference in their bodies and mine. I had practically given up being an altar boy, because of the feelings of hypocrisy I carried around with me. I still prayed to my friend God, but not as intensely as before. It was more of an insurance policy for whatever the future and eternity may have in store for me.

I started at St. Ethelburga's Roman Catholic Comprehensive in Barking. It was about a ten mile journey there and ten mile back everyday, this time by bus, from outside The Merry Fiddlers pub in Dagenham, to near Barking station. The Protestant schools were just around the corner, more modern, better equipped and near. The school was an old Victorian building and the facilities were abysmal. The playground had large ball-shaped lumps in the tarmac, where it had swelled up after being so badly laid. This made it really difficult to play football, or any kind of sport, which put us at a total disadvantage when we had to play other schools. The toilets were outside, green-tiled and cavernous with a long bench of wood with holes cut in it and it was a feat worthy of a British Commando to sit on it in winter to have a poo. There were basic facilities for scientific research, a couple of bunson burners, no facility for artwork or metalwork or woodwork.

Most of the time we would be marched to nearby Protestant schools to do these subjects. We did a lot of walking and not a lot of learning as far as I can remember. There were eight classrooms, all set around a large hall, four full of Catholics and four full of Protestants, a lively mix. 'Catholics all make you sick,' they cried. 'Proddy dogs are just like frogs,' we replied.

I spent an uneventful four years going backwards and forwards on London transport, for a time, without the need to drag my kid brother with me. Then he left the primary school and my duty at having to get us both to school started all over again.

I was an intense child and I am still intense as an adult. I trusted in people and institutions and things. I was, and am still, very sensible, perhaps too much so. My deep-rooted insecurities were born out of my sense of responsibility to my family and the burden of looking after other people. It was a burden I accepted because that is what I was taught to do by family, school, religion. On the shoulders of one so young this sense of responsibility nurtured a steely resolve to become accomplished and successful and to despise unfairness and injustice.

4. East-End Characters

I started going to pubs as soon as I could pass for old enough because that was where the music was. This was 1954, pre-Rock & Roll, and I would hang around the jazz clubs listening to Tubby Hayes, Bert Courtley, Joe Harriott and also Ted Heath and Jack Parnell. My life was totally taken up with music and, although I couldn't read music, I had a solid golden ear so sang in tune and swung like a cool dude.

I knocked around with a crowd who were all young, talented and as hip and cool as could be. I noticed that if you wanted to be in the 'in-crowd' you had to have something to set you apart from everyone

else. At my local pub, The Fiddlers in Dagenham, all the prominent faces hung around at the right hand side of the bar. They were all the notorious faces in the area: minor

The Fiddlers 1918

villains, duckers and divers with wads of money and lots of life. Some were forty years old and I deduced even then that, if I didn't get a move on, that's where I would end my days. That wasn't what I wanted: I had my sights set on greater things.

My brother and I would go along to all the talent nights, jazz nights and sing-along nights. Although I was rather shy, I pushed myself like mad to get on stage. My brother was far from shy and was out day and night meeting people and grafting in the market, helping any of the chaps that needed a hand to do anything to earn a 'Sov'. He was a real go-getter and made a career of networking as much as possible, I was more retiring and having Patrick as my brother helped me out in meeting people. So, what would perhaps have taken twenty years of going to the pub, my brother and I accomplished in three: we became part of the right-hand side of the bar by the time I was seventeen and my brother was fifteen and a half. We were in with the big guys because we were able to sing with some style and grace and we were adopted as singing mascots. We sang all the standards and the jazzers: *'Go Brisy, Sing'*, *'The Lady is a Tramp'*, *'Bewitched, Bothered and Bewildered'*, *'Go Patsy'*, *'My Mother's Eyes'*, *'My Yiddishe Momme'*. We would bring the house down whenever we sang. A Sunday morning session at The Fiddlers was the funniest, greatest place on earth. Everyone was in the mood to have the best time they could in the few hours that the pub was open. We all met up and told the stories of what we had been up to the night before: the girls we had tried to pull, the scrapes we had got into, the Chinese meals we had eaten on the steps in Limehouse. We would go to Chinese restaurants after coming out of the pub, the gags would be flying, I would take particular heed of where my brother was sitting and if it was near the door I knew he was going to do a runner. Not wanting to get stuck with a bill for ten hungry drunks as soon as I saw him twitch at the end of the meal I would be off close on my kids' heels, leaving the rest of the guys fighting to get through a narrow

29

door-way so as not to get stuck with the bill. We would be sprinting up the road laughing like hyenas followed by little Chinamen armed with knives and choppers.

It is difficult to describe the feeling of youth and high spirits we grew up with. The times were changing like they never had before. Young people were being catered

Jon's mates shared their exploits, Jon 5th from the left

for like never before: we had our own music and fashions for the first time ever, and we had a voice in Rock & Roll. I never completely bought into Rock & Roll, because I had always listened to all the old Blues and Gospel singers like Muddy Waters and Big Bill Broonzy and I knew that this new music wasn't so new really. I was born a little too early to be into the likes of a three-chord, hip-swinging, white dude called Elvis, or some skinny college boys singing in a cut-glass accent called The Stones. I really considered this new music second class. Nonetheless, when The Beatles and The Stones were becoming famous, it was impossible to ignore the change in the scene. I was stuck to performing to the cool school, the old ways of music and life that I loved.

The Fiddlers on a Sunday morning would have a young band, Brian Poole and the Tremelos, and young guys all gigging to get into groups, The Dave Clarke Five as well as would-be members of The New Faces and lots of the other Essex and London bands. The atmosphere was absolutely electric, and the consumption of alcohol in just a couple of hours of drinking time was incredible. The place would be jam-packed and the scene was set for unadulterated fun. It was such a thrill hearing a song that had never been performed before, sung by about three hundred happy-go-lucky young guys.The first time the whole room sang *"She loves you, yeah, yeah, yeah!"* was amazing. It was glorious, hard-drinking, lads-together fun.

One day, in the middle of all this mayhem, a guy called Bootsie Brandon once rode into the pub on a white horse, dressed as a monk. He rode up to the bar and asked for a flagon of ale and a bale of hay for the horse, Tavener. Then, one Sunday, a guy called Teddy Green from East Ham challenged Bootsie from Romford to a duel. So help me, the word went around and the Sunday morning session took on an even more electric atmosphere. Teddy Green was coming from East Ham on a bus, dressed as Coco the Clown on roller skates. Bootsie was coming from Romford dressed in a ballerina's tutu with a bra and wig over a leotard – also on roller skates. They had timed it to arrive outside the pub simultaneously. Greeny got off the Number 87 and Bootsie got off the Number 25, having had a long journey on the long seat of the bus, impervious to the looks of the other passengers. This was the meeting of two of the biggest pranksters in the pub and it was billed as the showdown at The Fiddlers Corral. Greeny got off on one side of the road all clowned-up with a large gamp umbrella. Bootsie got off on the other side of the road tutu-ed up and holding a large ham bone. The two met in the middle of the road and, watched by all the guys from the pub, they skirted around each other on their skates and thrust and parried into a dual to the comedy death, who was to be top dog funster at the notorious Fiddlers. The crowd went wild with laughter and the traffic was brought to a standstill. People in cars and buses and those standing outside the pub were in fits of laughter as the two nutters dualled on skates. The band in the pub relayed the loudest rendition of *'Johnny B. Goode'* ever played and the scene was indescribable.

The same pack instincts applied when we went to dancehalls like The Palais. You had to get into the right hand corner of the ballroom or you were no-one. In that corner were real tough faces from the East End of London, heavy duty villains, plus boxers, footballers, film stars, all young and up and coming. The Lazerus family from Chadwell Heath, thirteen brothers who were mostly professional boxers, were definitely some of the chaps. They were called The Lazars. Lew Lazar was middle-weight champion of Great Britain and a black cab driver. Some of his older brothers had been prominent boxers and street scrappers too. The one I knew the best was Mark Lazar - he was the single most talented person I had ever met then. At eighteen he could box to a professional standard, he could play football to the same degree, he could sing up a storm and tell jokes and dance and street fight like a movie star. Jimmy Greaves was part of the bunch, as was the up and coming Kathy Kirby, Bobby Moore, Martin Peters, Terry Downes and Billy Walker who was bouncer on the door along with Lee Hicks, a Joe Palooka lookalike and Kenny Lynch and his sister Maxine.

Phil Tate and his big band, a twenty piece orchestra and The Geoff Rowena Quartet, played great live music every night of the week save Monday when we had records. This was 1957, Rock & Roll was just starting, and I couldn't wait to get home from work and get to The Fiddlers, have a few drinks, and then get to The Palais.

Then one day Mecca, the company that owned The Palais, employed a new manager. There used to be some sharp turnarounds in managers, because there were some monumental battles among the different gangs. It was after the Canning Town gang had an almighty fight in which I saw one guy pull a Japanese sword from inside his jacket and trousers and lop off some guy's ear and someone got thrown off the balcony, that Mecca employed a manager the likes of which we had never seen. Remember these were staid ballroom dancing days some days of the week and here was this new guy with his hair dyed all different stripes of colour: he was called Jimmy Savile. Jimmy injected a new atmosphere into the place and the entertainment quotient soared. We would try any way we could to beat the system, to get in for free. A group of around thirty of us would meet in *The Havelock Pub* opposite The Palais. We would club our money together and a few guys would pay to go in The Palais.

Inside they would strongarm some kids for their tickets, bring them over to The Havelock where the more deft and light-fingered of the crowd would make holes in the collected tickets with pointed matches, to count as pass-outs. Jimmy Savile would cotton on to this and would change the punches that made the holes in the tickets. But I knew a girl who worked in the stationery department at Fords and she got me a punch with an alternating head which put us ahead of the game, which for me was a minor result.

We would make forays out of our own manor and go to *The Royal* at Tottenham looking for some new blood. It could be quite hairy when the local guys saw a team of us coming onto their ground and some real fights happened. The same went for The East Ham Town Hall, where we would go dancing to Bill Birch and his band. We'd also go to The Royal Mount at Chingford and The Plaistow Townhall: great music, great dancing, lots of beer and a fight thrown in. Rock & Roll was on the way, things could only get better.

I was working at Ford Motor Company earning about £8 a week, after I gave my mother £3, there was not a lot left to get through the week. So I used to work in Romford Market on a Saturday, from 6.30 in the morning to about 9 at night to get a bit of extra beer money. I was really conscientious and always got there on time, did a good day's graft, did not fiddle a penny and picked up a couple of quid, which was a life saver and really went a long way. My brother always told me what a mug I was for caring so much. 'You gotta fuck 'em,' he would say. 'They think you're at it anyway, so you might as well nick a bit for yourself. How do you think they got a start? Definitely not by being as caring as you are and hoping the boss would bung them a bit more. No, it's the opposite: they think you're at it anyway and they don't trust you anyway, so fuck 'em.'

'If I knew who 'they' were,' I would say, 'I *would* fuck 'em. But I don't, so who are they?'

'Them' he would say. 'All of them. Anyone who uses you and doesn't pay you your true worth, so fuck 'em.'

'Fuck who?' I would say and so it would go on and on.

As I say, I started in the market at six in the morning but my kid brother started at ten. His day at work was very different to mine.He would walk past me on the greengrocer's stall that I was working on and he would tut, laugh and call me a mug. He was known to all and sundry, a real *Jack the Lad* and the stallholders would call to him as he passed: 'Patsy, here boy'

'Morris, my son. What's up?' he would ask, all innocent.

'Give us a break for a tea and a piss, Patsy. I'll be back in about half an hour if I can get a bet on.'

'Sure Mo, no hurry'

Soon as Mo had left, my kid had had a deuce pound out of the till in his bin and proceeded to make it up in short change and short measure, till Mo came back and gave him five Bob.

And so it would go all up the market. He would be finished by five and in the pub and when I walked in at nine after a long day's work, he would call me a mug again. We would laugh and get pissed and get up and sing. The difference was that I would have two quid and a bag of fruit and he would have about a score.

Then one day the dreaded green card arrived on the doormat: *Your presence is requested to attend a medical for two year's National Service.* This card struck terror into the hearts of all the guys I knew, guys who were in the prime of youth. The government, who had not done a lot for the likes of working boys like me, now wanted me to donate two years of my life marching and painting bits of coal white. It was time to get my thinking cap on if I was going to get out of National Service. With my brother's 'Fuck 'em' ringing in my ears, I gingerly made my way to Wanstead Army Medical Centre. I had done my best to catch a cold by getting really pissed on black rum at Johnny Cate's party on a frosty November night. I'd fallen asleep under a bush and woke covered in frost and suffering with almost hyperthermia. I dragged myself to the medical the next day feeling close to death, hungover and wheezing. I stripped off in a line of ten guys and was checked for deformities. The doctor touched my scrotum and asked me to cough. I croaked and he told me I wasn't supposed to enjoy it. He put a stethascope to my chest and back to have a closer listen to the creaking and wheezing in my chest. I had three separate medicals and I failed the last one on sinusitus. For once in my life I had fucked 'em, but in hindsight I wish I hadn't; I think it would have made me grow up a lot quicker.

It says something for the ingenuity of the crowd I knocked around with, but out of about thirty guys, only six did their National Service and some of those guys who failed were as fit as it was possible to be, considering all the scrapping that was going on everywhere we went.

Billy Walker and Lee Hicks were bouncers on the door of The Ilford Palais. Though they were two massive guys, it was not an easy place to be on the nights when the pubs turned out and everyone was up for a great night of dancing and pulling birds. They had some almighty scraps on the door repelling rival gangs and anyone else who would try to gib in. They worked in Billingsgate fish market and the story goes that they put the suits they were going to their army medical in, in a barrel of soused herrings, dried them off and wore them to the Medical Centre for their medicals. Picture these two huge guys in suits that had shrunk and stank of fish. They did an Acadamy award-winning portrayal of characters from a classic war film and expressed the wish to get into battle as soon as possible. It appears they were failed on diminished responsibilty. They resumed their dapper massive presence at The Palais and were lauded as heroes for their acting prowess. Billy Walker went on to be heavyweight champion of Great Britain. We were all in The Havelock pub when Billy KO-ed a huge American heavyweight, when he represented England as an amateur and England beat the Yanks ten bouts to nil. The pub went wild and someone started a fight.

About 1959, Rock & Roll was in full swing and the dance scene was beginning to change. Mecca was changing its policy of live music and the bands tried hard to compete with the new music. I was twenty by then and we were Mods, three-button, mohair-suited, shining like deep blue beacons in the night. Some of the gang were getting famous playing football, boxing, thieving. There were some heavy duty faces in the crowd now. There were loads of jobs to be had, but this crew didn't just want jobs to make money, it took too long and didn't come quick enough. They wanted to be famous. It dawned on me too that I needed to make some moves to secure a future that had not looked too bright when I left school with not one creditable certificate.

I've never thought that any of the guys I grew up with were stupid. In fact, they were smarter than most, but just not part of the mainstream. We were not bad but eager to do whatever it took to get out of the no-hope pigeonhole we had been put in. Whether it's through lack of facilities or motivation, it is almost a gaurantee that if a fertile brain isn't engaged, then there is every chance that what starts off as boyish pranks almost certainly goes on to some kind of villainy. I saw it happen. My saving grace was that my mate God had given me the ability to sing, God bless him, and that saved my life.

I was singing at *The Cubana* in Ilford which was owned by the English equivalent of Liberace, but without the candelabra and diamond suits. Nevertheless, Jackie Wilson was a fast-playing flamboyant jazzer. The place was the height of cool. I remember seeing a skinny-looking guy named Cliff Lawrence who looked just like Frank Sinatra in his early years, but who sounded just like Mel Torme. Shit, was he cool, dragging on a cigarette and singing cool jazz. The crowd was really hip and there was a mixture of villains and well-known faces. I looked as sharp a greyhound, six-foot, lean and slick, my material was strictly standards leaning heavily on Sammy Davis Jnr. material.

One of the pubs I sang in was *The Dudragon* in Hackney. Now I am talking England,London, East-end B.F.P.C.O. (before poofs came out). Gays were all low-key. We all had a teacher that seemed to take more than a healthy interest in getting you to stay behind after school and join the young Catholics boys club,or had a relative who was in the merchant navy and would squeeze your leg, give you a sweet and talked with a lisp. But at the Dudragon the room was full of the most well-dressed funny, talented, all singing, all dancing gay men and women. Not all lipstick and dresses, I'm talking Saville Row suited, Hollywood film star *Rock Hudson* types. *Billy, Gay, Bobby* these were the comperes and entertainers. Sylvie the Lesbian,what-ever that was? She wore tight leather trousers some-one said *"Hey Sylv how'd you get into those pants"*. *"You can start with a gin and tonic"* she would say. Everyone had a quick wit and a lot of class. They held the stage and sang up a storm, they gagged to die for, they ripped the piss out of all and sundry and God forgive you if you tried to get smart or took offence. The room was also full of heavy faces and people who weren't regulars and didn't know the scene would be severely dealt with. I was fresh-faced and slightly naive about what exactly these guys got up to. All I knew was to be around them meant there would be great music and laughs, like you could not find anywhere else. They liked me and never threatened me or my masculinity.

39

I also worked at *The Ranchhouse*, a night-club in Ilford made from timber. This was a really great place, terrific swinging live music with *Kenny Clayton* on piano and the best British sidesmen sitting in. The crowd would have well-known East End faces, including the *Kray* twins. The West Ham football team would use the club and drop in after training, so you'd often see famous footballers like Noel Cantwell, Malcolm Allison, Malcolm 'Mussy' Musgrove and John Bond. They were real characters. After training they would come in for drink and then the fun would really start! Good food, great music and lots and lots of laughs.

What I learned from all these great characters was a sense of my place. I learnt not to get flash because there was always someone who might not have the front that you had and if they thought you took yourself too seriously then they might think you needed a good slapping, just to let you know that just because you could sing a few songs up on a stage, that didn't count for too much if you were not just a little humble with it. I learned to be modest and unassuming and I was liked for it, so that if anyone who I didn't know took offence to me there were people who would look after me.

You had to be cool, or you could get really hurt. It was all done in such a low-key way, you just would not know if trouble was coming your way even though you considered yourself aware of the game. Being on stage, singing songs, meant that the girls thought you were really smooth and would sometimes show out to you. But if some guy had picked her out as his, even though he had not made a move on her, you could get into serious trouble. He might have been working up to it for several weeks and just because of a few songs, you had crashed in straight away, right into the deep shit and with a lot of diplomacy, to keep the face pretty, you'd drop a few names and graciously retreat. This permeated all East End society and ignorance of it, in the higher echelons of the East End could get you into serious trouble, just by a look, a gesture - it didn't take much so you had to know how to handle yourself. It made the atmosphere electric and exciting.

I was doing the rounds, and I had got a little reputation for singing some good toons. Others in my groups were doing well for themselves too: Billy Walker was getting well-known; Kathy Kirby had hit the big-time, Bobby Moore, Geoff Hurst and Martin Peters were playing for West Ham; Jimmy Greaves was a star; Les Allen was getting well-known as was Terry Venables. Marky Lazar had decided to choose football out of all the things he was good at and any amount of other minor faces were getting picked up for sport and other ways of getting famous and I was knocking myself out trying to get on.

As the crowd was going off to do other things, I got in with a crowd of guys from Seven Kings. The main guy was a little whizzer named Terry Clements. His family owned a car site in Seven Kings. It was about a quarter of a mile long, full of cars. He, his brother Tony, and his Mum and Dad ran Seven Kings Autos and they were white hot at car sales. One Christmas Terry, who was only about twenty, bought his dad a Silver Cloud Rolls Royce and his mum and himself a Fleetwood Cadillac apiece, just like the ones in the Elvis Presley movies. Eddie Pillar was a bookie, Johnny Braine's family had a haulage business, Ernie Felgate's family also had a haulage business, Phil Lee, a pencil-thin charmer ruined to death by his doting parents. They all had bundles of dough and I was earning about a tenner a week at Fords and anything else I could pick up from my singing gigs. They had all become well-known for their high spending locally and in the West End. I didn't have that sort of money to spend but the fact that I could sing made me a place in the group. Phil Lee took me under his wing and I spent a lot of time with his family. Eddie Pillar was twenty going on sixty with all the mannerisms of someone much older and was called the General. Johnny Braine had been run over by one of his dad's lorries and had nearly died, so he did not give a shit about anything. He came from a family of pranksters and roared around London in a red Sunbeam Tiger which went like shit off a shovel. Me and the other guys would go to his house absolutely suited and booted in one of Jack Bunney's hand-cut, tailor-made suits, three-buttoned mohair, tight-fitting, sleek as could be. We would walk up to the Braines' house like the rat pack and ring the doorbell, then *whoosh*, his Dad would throw a bucket of water over us and the whole family would piss themselves laughing at the bedraggled mess standing outside their door.

We would go to all the local country clubs and classy night clubs in Essex or the West End: *The Astor, Dorothy's Club* in Knightsbridge, *The Bagatelle*. More times than not when we went to

The Bagatelle, we would walk in and over in the corner a man would have two girls with him and if there was a violin player at the table, Terry would know his dad was in. We would get a table as far away as possible and have a great night until the bill came round and Terry's dad always worked his bill onto Terry's table.

We had some absolutely fantastic times. In 1957, we drove to Spain in a brand new yellow Chevrolet convertable, the likes of which turned heads everywhere we went. We drove down through France and into Spain, where they were using donkey carts and Model T. Fords to get around in. We went wild in Barcelona on *Las Ramblas*.

This was Franco's Spain and a thousand pesetas could buy you the moon. We sang, danced, got drunk and made love for two incredible weeks and on the way home

Barcelona trip: L to rt. Terry Clements, Jon Jon, Johnny Braine,   Far Right: Eddie Pillar

crashed the car into a ditch, doing extensive damage to the offside of the car and splitting the battery. Trying to get a replacement for a Ford

Poplar would have been a feat, but for an American Chevrolet in 1957 was impossible. All the stops were pulled out and the A.A. got us a battery and we limped home. We exchanged that car for a sky blue Lincoln Covertable, it was the dogs' bollocks. Ernie Felgate had a souped up Standard Vanguard with the snub front and the round back, Johnnie Braine had use of a Wolseley 4/44, the same model as the police used and we got some peaked caps and nicked some Red X bottles that we would fill with pee, flag down cars, pull up along side, get the occupants to wind down the windows, and squirt them with piss, and toe it out of there as quick as possible.

Eddie Pillar's brother's girlfriend's dad, Mr Jack Bowen, took a fancy to my singing and would invite me to some of his big house parties. He would introduce me as his protégé and I would sing for everyone He arranged for me to have some singing lessons with a Mr Douglas Hemmings in East Ham. I had seriously made up my mind to get out of Ford and Dagenham before it was too late.Making the time to go for singing lessons was tough. It interfered with my social life and it felt very strange going to East Ham on a Tuesday night for a one hour lesson, with this old man who was seventy-three then and with the other pupils as straight as could be. But I was determined. My kid brother was curious to know where I went every Tuesday and I would make up some excuse and not let on, otherwise I would have had the piss taken out of me something bad.

I went week in, week out practicing my scales and breathing, feeling as though it was too namby-pamby and I wasn't improving.

But I was so determined not to be left behind as all the people around me were getting rich and famous. I realised I had only my singing to make the life I had promised for myself and I knew that only hard work could make it come true. I remember going to the cinema and the thrill and surprise of watching James Dean who was the same age as me, portraying all the confusion and angst of an eighteen year old. Most of our heroes were much older than we were and, although we enjoyed and admired them, it was only when the likes of James Dean, *Pier Angoli, Natalie Wood* come on the screen, that I knew it was possible for me to make it too. The problem was how?

5. East-End to West-End

One day I picked up a newspaper at Mr Hemming's place, one that I had never seen before. It was called *The Stage*. It was a theatrical paper and it had lists of credits, criticisms and, best of all, advertisements for professional jobs in London and the rest of the country. My singing lessons paved the way for a career, but if I hadn't have gone to lessons, I would not have found this new way of getting into full-time showbiz.

I answered an advertisement for an audition to join a vocal group. The audition was at Weeke's Studio in Hanover Square in the West End. I took a fast song, *'Hello Young Lovers'*, and a ballad, 'Bewitched, Bothered and Bewildered', and got dressed to impress in a tailor-made Jack Bunney special three-buttoned suit. The group of people that were waiting to be auditioned looked like something out of *The Vagabond King*, pukka theatricals. I stepped into the waiting room and felt really out of place and it was all I could do to make myself stay because I was unlike anybody who was waiting to be auditioned. The door opened and a voice beckoned the next auditionee in. The door had a frosted glass window and through it I could hear a voice asking what experience he had had. The campest voice I've ever heard said, 'I've been resident in the West End doing shows for three years, understudy in *Carousel*, in the chorus in *Oklahoma*.' I began to get really nervous as they all seemed to have so much more theatrical experience than me and were all so gay.

I stopped being so nervous when this silhouette with an out-stretched arm kept gliding past the frosted glass singing in the campest high falsetto voice, 'There is nothing like a dame, nothing in the world.' It was all I could do not to burst out laughing, so I bit my lip and his rendition was brought to a halt in mid chorus. 'Thank you, that's just fine,' a voice said. 'It's a nice voice but not exactly what we are looking for.' The door opened and the vision stepped out: 'No luck, Beverly?'

'No hun. I think they want fucking Nat King Cole...' in white! See you hun'

Then the voice called me in. It was make or break. I stepped into the room and saw three ordinary looking guys sitting behind a table at the end of the room. They smiled and said 'Good to meet you. What have you got to sing for us?' I had seen a nod from one to the other, on the way I looked, so it seemed to be going well even before I had sung a note. I placed the music in front of the pianist, who asked what tempo I wanted it played in. The song had been written as a ballad but I had been singing it in a fast four, just like I had heard it recorded by Buddy Greco. The pianist's name was Clive Chaplin – he was a noted piano player in the West End theatre and nightclub scene. He played a four bar intro and I swung into 'Hello Young Lovers'. I really sang it well and, as I soared to a high driving finish, I didn't want the experience to come to an end. The three guys clapped and Clive congratulated me, on being the first one today with any kind of musical soul, not just a dancer trying to sing. I prepared to start the

47

ballad, I was looking forward to singing with the pianist again, but a one of the men said, 'That's not necessary. I think by your style and musical ability, you are just what we are looking for.' After a sharp intake of breath, the guys beckoned me to the table, we shook hands. They told me that good manners meant they were duty-bound to listen to the rest of the gay Cavaliers sitting in the outside room. We agreed to meet in the cafe next door to the studio as soon as they had finished with the other half dozen hopefuls eager to get out of the chorus.

I made my way downstairs, past studios full of the most wonderful voices, most of them operatic or the type you would hear in a West End musical and pinched myself at the thought of maybe joining the elite of the West End theatre. Me, a Cockney kid with an difficult past, standing on the threshold of who-knew-what. I sat in the cafe marvelling at some of the well-known faces coming and going from the studios. Radio, TV, film and West End actors, comics and singers, people I had only dreamed of being like, let alone being in their company. The journey from the East End of London to the West End of London was, for me and guys like me, the longest twenty miles on the planet.

When the three guys and Clive came in, we all shook hands and ordered tea and sarnies. 'We were glad to meet you,' they said. Apparently they had thought the day would be just as unsuccessful as the others days they had spent looking for the right singer. 'So, you got the job. How does it feel.?'

I was so unsure of myself and the job to come that I found myself saying, I wasn't sure. 'Don't get me wrong' I said, 'I am pleased to have got the job but the whole scene is new to me.' I told them a bit about my musical experiences and tastes and they seemed pleasantly surprised at my genuine naivety about theatre and performing on the legitimate stage.

And that was how I joined The Four Gale Boys. The other boys in the band were Colin, John and Mac. Colin was a happy-go-lucky fellow with an open gregarious personality from Plymouth in Devon. He had trained at the Guildhall School of Music and was a genuine Basso Profundo, a rich bass voice,. He seemed to overdo everything: eating, drinking, sex, and later,

The Gale Boys

drugs. Colin, a cuddly bear of a man. His lust for life was gigantic and with his warm Devonshire twang and the fact that he was hung like a horse, it was a handful to keep tabs on. He would end up in the most incredible situations. Lucas was from Rugby and very ginger, astute and condescending when sober, gregarious and cryptically funny when drunk. He sang bass in the group, even though Colin was the much better bass singer. Mac was from Birmingham, and his Tenor was beautiful. He couldn't read music but had been endowed with perfect pitch. So the harmonies in a four part group were Lucas as Bass, myself as Baritone, Colin as Second Tenor and Mac as High Tenor. John's vibrato was very suspect, so as we did some comedy material, he was given the job of carrying the humour in the programme. Mac's perfect pitch became a burden we all had to bear because, even though he didn't know what was musically wrong, it would scream in his ear, like fingers being dragged across a blackboard. Another problem was that he had been a member of the S.A.S., in Malaya, used to dropping from planes into the jungle with a ninety pound weight suspended from his leg, crashing into the jungle canopy and firing at terrorists. So it was not wise to upset him, as the supercilious Lucas was apt to do.

I had a good deal of say in the costumes, as I was a really snappy dresser, which was one of the attributes I brought to the group. I always thought it was awful to see acts - male or female - who had been sitting in their stage costumes making them look wrinkled and dishevelled before they got on stage. Shoes were another area of concern, because at stage level in cabaret, your shoes were just at eye-level and people noticed how well groomed you were by the state of your shoes. Of course, this was all before The Stones and The Faces and all the new groups decided to dress in tatty jeans and sweat shirts.

To keep his weight on an even keel Colin went to his G.P. and was prescribed Dexodrine. We didn't know it then but this was speed - an amphetamine, It would quicken up your metabolism and dull your appetite for food and sex. Colin's desire for food dropped, but his

50

need for alcohol and sex went up to new heights. He began to twich a lot, but balanced against his weight loss there was not much we could say. He once got locked in a nightclub in Darlington after we had finished the show. He was playing the fruit machine – something he did a great deal. Twitching away, he was oblivious to the fact that only the night lights had been left on and the place had been locked up and everyone had gone home. He lost all his money and Colin swears that as he turned to walk to the door to leave, an apparition in a ghostly form walked right through him. He said it was icy cold and it frightened the life out of him. He remained sober as a judge for all of four nights before he shook off the fear it had put into him.

Colin and John shared rooms together and the mess in their place was horrific. The air was always full of cigarette smoke, farts and feet. I shared with Mac and we kept our rooms clean and tidy, as neither he nor I smoked and we were rather more fastidious than the other two. My burden was that the slightest noise or a light would wake me and keep me awake. Mac loved to have a bet and more times than I care to remember, he would be propped up under his sheets with a bedside light, picking out the horses for the next day's bets.

My first task on joining the group was to learn my baritone parts in the four part harmony. Many of the arrangements were written by the very famous composer and arranger Peter Knight. He did arrangements for people like Sammy Davis Jnr. and they were the tops. Unfortunately my parents had got rid of our upright piano and all I had to work out my musical lines on was an accordian. Sweating over the notes, pumping the bellows out with one hand and stabbing out the relative notes on the music sheet, it couldn't have been more difficult but somehow I managed to learn my baritone parts.

We worked really hard on fabulous arrangements and produced a well-mixed musical act of about an hour and a half's material. We did fast numbers and soulful ballads as well as some a-cappella songs in the Four Freshman and Hi-Los style. The thrill of singing in four-part harmony, when the pitch and the intonation and the dynamics are spot on, cannot be surpassed by any other human experience. It feels the closest a human can get to God. But equally, if any of these neccessary ingredients is awry, it can be the most upsetting experience as well. It is so easy to go just off-key and sometimes, especially if we had been working live performaces and hadn't been into a recording studio for a while, we would find ourselves working our own lines too hard and not listening enough to the whole sound. Once we did a radio broadcast after we had been on the road for a long time and we were shocked at our lack of dynamics and intonation.

Then we got the gig to die for: a season at the world famous Windmill in Archer Street, Piccadilly, London. It was five shows a day. The first show was at 11 a.m. and the last show finished at 11 p.m. It felt a long way from working at a motor company as a minor member of a huge indiscriminate work-force to becoming part of a select group of people, that the public would pay to see.

As sharp and street-wise as Cockney geezers are supposed to be as portrayed by Michael Caine in Alfie, most guys I grew up with were rather slow in the *bird-pulling* stakes. Most of them were so busy looking right and acting in the true Hollywood style, concentrating on their immaculate clothes, hair and grooming and perfecting the chat. Definately not too pushy or flash,a cool, sylish approach built up over a long period of time. Some like Bootsie Brandon who looked like Ben Turpin out of the Keystone Cops, was not considered a menace to any man or beast and because of this Bootsie was not shy pulled a lot of birds and never suffered the pains of rejection. But if you did have your eye on a girl, you would have to walk across a dance floor that measured seventy-five yards wide by a hundred yards long to ask her for a dance. Imagine: there would be a beautiful girl in an Alma Cogan dress, beehive hair-do and stiletto shoes. You might have had your eye on her for weeks and this was the night you were going to make the long walk. After all the banter had settled with your mates who would be busy ripping the shit out you because you hadn't made a move on her, but had told everyone you were going to for weeks, this was the night. The longest walk in the world is across a dance floor just as the band is playing your favourite song. This is it - now or never - cutting through the crowd, away from your pals across the floor. The vision that you had been working yourself up for, was always accompanied by a little ugly bird with glasses. You would walk up to them and ask politely, 'Would you like to dance?' She would look at her ugly sidekick, they would both look back at you and giggle and say 'No thanks.' You would feel crushed, self preservation made you crack back, looking at the little girl " I was talking to Snow

White not one of the Dwarfs" That was only the half of it. You now had to get back to your own crowd, praying that no-one had seen what you had just endured. But someone always had. As you tried to slip back into the crowd a voice would say, 'Not a lover or a fighter, eh? Aye, there goes six weeks' hard work, more bashing the Bishop for you. Aren't your family worried about your masculinity?' They would take the piss something terrible.

It would make you question your ability to do the most natural of things, like pulling a bird. Not just any old girl, but good-looking birds – the ones that all of the guys would be after. Not many of them had the guts to make that long walk though and most of the guys ended up pulling their mate's sisters or cousins, or someone that a mate or a family member knew. It took so long to romance a girl that most of the guy's married the first girl they made love to on a regular basis; they married her in case they never got their oats again. That is why there were so many fights, the testosterone levels where at an all-time high.

Can you imagine how my life changed then when I started working at TheWindmill. This was the most famous theatre in the world for naked women. So here am I in the West End, getting paid more money than I had ever had, doing what I loved the most, singing surrounded by the most beautiful naked young girls. I thought I had died and gone to heaven. These were not tatty lewd girls, these were hand-picked Sheila van Damm starlets. They were feted by top members of society. But they were also very pleased that we would be working with them because, most of the men who courted their favours were much older and bought their company. Whereas we were young and fun and in the same business. We had it made.

It's been told by anyone who worked at The Windmill about the antics of the audience. They paid 17 *s* 6 *d* and they could stay all day and watch all the performances. That meant that as the theatre opened for the first show, there would be a rush for the front seats. Throughout the day, a procession of people would be climbing over the seats to make their way to the front: as a seat was vacated, they would move from the back of the circle to the front of the

circle and then make their way downstairs and seat-hop between the shows hoping to get ever closer to the stage, to study ever closer these nubile young ladies in a static pose, or with feather fans, hoping upon hope to get a glimpse of you know what. Women in general were not easy to get to know and sex was a completely different set of rituals, especially in the East End, than it is today.

The shows included up-and-coming comedians and they would have to work so hard to get the proverbial titter from the audience.

Many of the countries comics like Bruce Forsyth, Peter Sellers, Harry Secombe learned their craft from this five show a day blood-letting. We didn't fare any better: four young, good-looking, well-dressed guys, bounding on stage with 'Sing Hallelujah'. An audible groan would go around the auditorium as we broke into an unaccompanied version of 'Shenandoah' and the whole stalls became a mass of newspapers, as the men lifted them to read until the girls came back on. I could not have worked in a better place to learn my craft. The Van Damms who owned the theatre were hard taskmasters, but I learned so much about the movement, acting, singing and music and about showbiz in general.

Once the gang back home found out where I was working I became the toast of the town. My brother said what a sneaky git I was going for singing lessons but his kudos rose when he told people his brother was in showbiz in the West End. My greatest gift was to invite my mother and father to the show and see their faces when they realised one of their boys had started in the big time.

The scene outside *The Windmill* on a Monday morning in Archer Street, is a scene that is no longer repeated. It was where all the professional musicians would meet, an open-air gathering of the most talented people working in and around London or from abroad. The atmosphere was electric, the hubble-bubble of stories and laughter filled the whole street; there was nowhere else like it in the world and I was a part of it. The conversations were truly incredible, all the inside stories of what was going on in the West End theatre, cabaret and concert tours. Musicians tended to be treated as second class citizens and so they became the world's greatest cynics. Their stories of the artistic foibles and the inadequacies of some of the big stars, was magic to listen to. I pinched myself constantly as I listened to musicians who had just finished a tour with Frank Sinatra, Nat King Cole, Ella Fitzgerald, Tony Bennett and on and on.

The cynical cryptic humour was of a kind you wouldn't hear anywhere else. The meanness of the top stars and orchestra leaders. Although the *musos* may have had a bitter experience at these peoples hands they were always able to turn it into a funny story told as well if not better than comics. Such a joke as a call across Archer Street" Hymie or Solly mouthing 'Can you do a night depping for me at the Savoy with Jack Hylton, how much?" impossible to hear above the noise Hymie would indicate how much by putting three fingers up to his lapel indicating three quid for the night. They would meet the next week Solly would say"You crook you said it was three quid, No said Hymie £2.50, two fingers and a thumb, you brock!

I spent six months in London visiting new-found musician friends, watching other artists, networking and learning and getting laid and partying like never before. I was going back to my old crowd less and less, because of all the time spent rehearsing and grafting. Some of the guys came up to town and I introduced them to people I was working with. In most cases my real friends that I had grown up with treated me the same and could be relied upon still. Ours was a

57

genuine friendship, that wouldn't be broken, no matter who or what you were.

6. On The Road -
Entertaining US Troops in Germany

We were coming to the end of the season at *The Windmill* when we were approached by an agent who wanted to book us for some shows in Germany singing on the American bases. We passed an audition and got fixed up with a tour of Germany for four months. The American Forces nightclubs were as

good if not better than Las Vegas nightclubs. The American Government spared not a penny in making their boys feel comfortable away from home. Acts from all over the world had to audition for the individual camp entertainment officers. You did a shortened version of your act and was awarded marks for suitability for camps all over the American sector of Germany. Frankfurt, Wiesbaden, Stuttgart, Heidelberg; so many places and so well paid. The entertainment facilities had to have a German representative and most of the agents were German. They were raking in money hand over fist, getting a budget from the American entertainment managers and beating down the price to the act. Fortunes were being made and the acts knew it; there was an air of disgruntlement. We had been living in the fast lane and there wasn't a lot of spare cash about, so we were at the point of being desperate. It must have shown because we were fighting hard to get some decent money from the bookers. When they smelt that you needed the money, they would beat the price down.

We all lived in designated professional digs and from there you auditioned for shows and waited for the call from the agent. I met a comedy ventriloquist from South Africa who had only been able to pick up a couple of shows a week and he couldn't save enough money to get back home. He was going stir crazy and used to walk around doing all the Walt Disney voices, all the time.

We would be driven out to the countryside to the army base in the depths of winter in an American army bus with no heating and very little suspension. Arriving at the camp, cold and hungry, we would make our way to the most palatial well-equiped nightclub you've ever seen. We would do the band call and prepare for the show.

We had a varied show of show music, spirituals and comedy. Having the correct material was so important. We thought that being an American audience they would appreciate The Four Freshmen and The Hi-Lo's material that we had been rehearsing for an American audience. How wrong we were. Some of the guys had never been out of their home state, some didn't know where Germany was or why they had been sent there by Uncle Sam, some had never had a pair of boots on and now they had a gun...

One golden mistake we made was not knowing about the racial divide there was in the army or the clubs we were about to entertain in. We walked out to one club and there was a perfect divide down the hall, all the blacks on the left side, all the whites on the right. We noticed it but paid it no heed not being too conversant at that time with the American racial divide. It came heavily to bear when Colin started into what we thought was a famous old American spiritual, 'Old Man River'. He came to the line "You and me, we sweat and slave, body all achin' and wracked with pain" when I saw the biggest black guy stand up. He was about six foot eight with a Little Richard hair-do. 'What the fuck do you know about sweatin' and strainin', you white honky pigs?' he yelled. I just managed to push Colin out of the way as a bourbon glass came whistling through the air, whilst still managing to keep singing as the glass crashed to the stage floor. With that, the right-hand side of the room crossed the divide between the two racial groups and a humungous riot started. Being staunch Englishmen, we stood our ground and continued singing as a tiny lieutenant followed by several huge military policemen loosed two rounds into the ceiling. At this point, the backing group broke into 'Show Me the Way to Go Home' and we left the stage. It was like a scene from *The Blues Brothers*.

The standard of artists appearing in the clubs was of the highest calibre: Sammy Davis Jnr., Count Basie, some of the biggest names in the business but they were often not known to the soldiers who they were sent to entertain. In the depths of a German winter we were doing a show with a gay and lesbian dance act called Valery and Tamara - Valery was the man. They argued incessantly about all things musical. Then there was a Jewish hypnotist, drummed out of Israel for doing press-ups on his female patients. We were a motley crew. We had great musical arrangements but some of the bands we needed for backing us were really not up to the task.

We fought our way through snow drifts to outlying camps all over the American sector of Germany. Some camps gained terrible reputations for the way they recieved the acts, some with very good reason. Some were bad. One camp, Bombholder, had a story about a soldier who had shot a waitress because she didn't get him a beer quick enough. This was exaggerated, as rumours can be, and got turned into a story about an act who had been shot at and killed. Every performer from then on was waiting for a gun to go off in their act. One act, an impressionist, was in the middle of his show when a tank back-fired and, before you could say 'BOO', he had run off stage and could not be encouraged to leave the tour bus no matter what. We were appearing in Heidelberg, Shape headquarters (Supreme Headquarters Allied Command Europe) with five-star generals and all the top brass. Valery and Tamara had a screaming fit and, as we were changing behind a screened-off area in the main room, Valery's voice got higher and higher and he tried to shoot Tamara with a starting pistol that they used in a Flamenco dance they did. *Bang! Bang!* You can just imagine the uproar in the room as two shots rang out. Once again the military policemen surrounded the screened-off area and we came out with our hands up pleading innocence as Valery and Tamara kept saying 'It was a accident, honest.' Our show was received with great applause. The Doc, as we called the hypnotist, did his act and the night was a success. We were all invited back to a top General's house for a party. No expense was spared on the American forces in Germany. The party was in full swing and we were all engaged in coversation with some of the top brass in Europe. Mac had made a play for the General's daughter who unfortunately Doc fancied too. Mac took the girl into the kitchen, followed some minutes later by Doc. After a short period of time, Mac came out of the kichen mesmerised. It turns out Doc had put the influence on him and was busily working on the girl!

Doc was so good at hypnosis that none of us would look him in the eyes. His next trick was to hypnotise a colonel and he had him suspended between two chairs, the back of his head on one and the heels of his feet on the other, six feet between the two and the colonel as stiff as a board between the two chairs. Doc then stood on his stomach and in broken English said 'And zo we see the power of hypnosis and all its facets!' The colonel's wife whispered in my ear, 'Does he know what he is doing? Only my husband has a slipped disc...'

We spent Christmas on Wurtzberg station. We had just finished three wild shows, transported hundreds of miles between them in a cold army bus. Sweating profusely after each show, jumping on a bus driving through snow drifts to the next show, we finished the last show at an officers' club in Wurtzburg. The officers' clubs were a cut above the ordinary soldiers' clubs and God knows they were better equiped than any nightclub in the UK. We needed some refreshment that wasn't a hamburger or a doughnut so we asked the driver to take us to a German place of entertainment. Everything in Germany closes down on Christmas night and the only place open was the railway station. The railway station was awash with Germans who had no families and American G.I.s who were all far from home and three sheets to the wind. We ate *Chinkin mit spiegel* (chicken with something) washed down with steins of beer. We were recognised by some of the G.I.s and they requested some songs. We were only too happy to comply with the request - not to do so would have been unwise and the crowd could have turned uglier than it already was. We sang an unaccompanied version of 'Shenandoah' in four-part harmony and it was received with tumultuous applause from the G.I.s and loud shouts from the German station staff that singing was *verboten in der station*. This fell on deaf ears and, to rile the staff even further, Doc was busy hypnotising soldiers to stand on the table and sing Christmas carols. The staff were going crazy as the room was filled with soldiers on tables hypnotised and singing at the tops of their voices. We were all screaming with laughter as Doc scurried around hypnotising all and sundry as waiters tried to pull the soldiers off the tables. The revelry was broken by an invasion of huge military policemen with their batons at the ready to break heads. Doc was instructed to bring the guys out of their trance and you should have seen the surprise on their faces as they awoke from singing 'Silent Night' to standing on the table wondering how they had got there. There were even more screams of laughter as the policemen brought order to their own troops and then it was brought to the attention of the captain that we were the ones who had instigated the whole situation. The captain rounded upon us and said that we could be in serious trouble for instigating a riot. With this, Lucas stood up, withdrew his passport from his jacket and thrust it under the captain's nose. The captain looked at the passport and told us that his great-grandparents came from Coventry and they would not have condoned such un-English behaviour. John then informed him in no uncertain terms and with the best cut-glass accent he could muster up, that his great-grandparents had never been stuck on bloody Wurtzberg station in the middle of a snowstorm on Christmas night far away from home. The room erupted with shouts and yells from the G.I.s and and the captain and his six military policemen quietly admonished us and asked kindly if we would leave to avoid any further aggravation. Having won the battle and lost the war we were escorted to the cold grey bus to take us back to Manheim, with the voices of the troops ringing in our ears.

The agents had practically had a blank cheque from the American government to keep the troops happy and they pulled all kinds of stunts to skim money off the acts. One of their ploys was, having enticed you to come to Germany, they either failed to put you in the showcases where the Army bookers chose the acts they wanted at their bases, or they skimmed the prices as well as taking a hefty commission. They might even keep you out of work so that you would accept a lesser fee just to pay for your living expenses. Between the bookers and the agents they made some serious money while the acts from all over the world just about made subsistance money. What you lacked in financial gain was more than made up for in experiencing all that could go wrong in learning your trade. That seeemed to be a constant occurance after all the years I spent learning my craft, someone always had the chance to skim something off the fees.

Germany was a real experience. We laughed, we starved, we fought and we indulged in wine, women and song. I was twenty years old and I was loving every minute of my life. It wasn't all rosy, sharing almost all your waking hours with three other guys who all had different ways of getting through life living in each others' pockets. It was tough. There were four different personalities, each with a separate, regional way of looking at things. Mac was Irish and had a temper that was strong enough to have got him into the S.A.S. in the Malayan jungle war. This was coupled with a beautiful Irish lyrical tenor with perfect pitch but with only a basic knowledge of music. This was a sure-fire recipe for disaster when we went to bandcalls and the pianist was not up to scratch and the piano was invariably out of tune. I spent so much time pulling Mac off musicians who were doing their best under very difficult circumstances and acting as mediator in his confrontations. John was from Rugby. He was not very talented with a faulty bass vibrato and a terrible supercilious attitude when sober, but cryptic and funny when drunk. We discouraged his drinking most of the time so as to keep his feelings of superiority over the rest of us, especially Mac. What an explosive mixture. Colin was from Devon. He was large, gregarious, warm, hugely talented in his musical ability and all-embracing in his attitude to wine, women and song. And finally, myself, a snappy East End Cockney and proud of it; cool, hip and the swinger of the group.

People wonder why really successful groups break up, when they seem to have everything going for them. It's because when you are performing all your individual petty habits are forgotten. As you perform as a group and especially whilst singing in close harmony, all the musical inflections, dynamics and intonations are blended to get the best sounds and performance. Away from the stage all your own petty little foibles come into play as you are subjected to the other group members' strange character traits. It's a fact that you only spent three to four hours in pursuit of achieving a good performance and twenty hours travelling to and from the gig, or finding a way of amusing yourselves.

What is so good about being in showbusiness is the total insecurity and extremes of good fortune and bad luck. A telephone call can change your whole life for good or ill. We received one such telephone call as we were coming to the end of an arduous and financially unsound five month contract hacking around the American sector of West Germany, the highlight of which was a gig in Berlin at the Wannsee, the top American headquarters only able to be reached with a trip through Checkpoint Charlie and a trip around the Berlin wall. This was 1961 at the height of the Cold War. Steel-eyed Russian soldiers scrutinised everything that we did. It was in the luxury of the officers' mess that we received a call from an agent in England for a one year season at Tito's nightclub in Palma de Mallorca. Life was about to change for the better.

7. Off to Majorca

What little money we had been able to save was used to buy tickets from the cold of a German winter to Palma de Majorca. Tito's was the best nightclub in the area with a thousand-seater open-air cabaret restaurant, perched on the edge of the sea at Magaluf. In the evening, the moon shone down onto the stage and it was a performer's idea of paradise. We were booked to perform here for the next year - heaven.

We arrived at Palma airport white, bedraggled and emaciated, carrying most of our belongings in an assortment of old bags. Colin was dressed in a huge, threadbare, brown Crombie overcoat that had served him well in a freezing winter but looked highly out of place in an azure, sun-filled sky. We were met by a mohair-clad, bronzed Victor Mature lookalike agent named Bob Weedon. Colin strode forward ignorant of what he must have looked like and shook Bob's hand. Having been brought up in the East End of London, I was able through experience to judge the look of absolute hidden horror on the agent's face. We looked a motley crew and he must have wondered what he had booked. I noticed this and, after we had all shaken his hand, I struck up a bell note in E flat, the guys picked it up immediately and, right there in the airport terminal we proceeded to sing in four-part harmony: "This is a lovely way to spend an evening. Can't think of anything I'd rather do. This is a lovely way to spend an evening. We want to save all our nights and spend them with you."

Bob was an agent and a musician too and the look on his face melted into a beaming smile. We were greeted then with great bonhomie by a chorus of applause and appreciation from all the people in the terminal building as Bob ushered us through the crowd like a very proud father.

We tumbled into the Bob's car. It was a golden Majorca day and we sped away to an awaiting array of influential club owners. We spilled out of the car in front of a beautiful house where a party was going on on the terrace around the pool. We were greeted over the ballustrade thirty feet up by some seriously rich-looking, stunning people and, to create a great impression immediately, Bob prompted us to sing the song we sang at the airport. This we did to another round of tumultuous applause.

Our ability to sing the most beautiful, unaccompanied musical harmonies took us out to be wined and dined all over the island, the whole time we were there. We were the feather in the cap of hosts and hostesses who wanted to add a golden touch to their parties. There was no-one else like us on the island and we milked it for all it was worth.

We were given an apartment to share while we settled in; rehearsals started the next day. We arrived at the club and were absolutely amazed at how stunning it was. We had to do a spot of our own for thirty minutes and also join in with some of the production numbers with all the dancers and other acts on the bill. The producer and choreographer was a fierce, black-haired, broad-shouldered, stunning-bodied Russian named Orloff with an equally stunning choreographer wife, Tamara. The dancers were from all over Europe, the pick of the bunch, able to do ballet, jazz, tap and all were tall and beautiful. Orloff took no time in impressing upon us how hard he expected us to work and made it clear that messing around with the dancers was not an option. We agreed wholeheartedly, ensuring him of our total professionalism and proceeded to kick in the old English Colditz mentality of not getting caught. Orloff was a hard taskmaster, able to reduce a brave man and girl to tears, which he often did, in the pursuit of a fantastic show. One hot, gruelling day, Orloff was really terse with all of us, standing onstage screaming at us for not being as sharp as he thought we should be with only days away before we opened the show. He ranted and, in the full heat of the day, stripped off his t-shirt to really show us all what he wanted us to do. Before anybody could pluck up the courage to tell him to put his t-shirt back on to cover up the obvious signs of someone embedding their nails into his back, the whole cast was treated to the spectacle of his wife running like a screaming banshee through the club to jump up on stage and severely assault him.

The opening was a resounding success and we were feted even more than before. I made a great friend of a six foot-four piano player named Phil Phillips. We called him the five-year-plan man, as he said without fail he would be in the top flight of British pianists within five years. He did it too, as I was later to work with him at The Talk of the Town in London's Leicester Square where he had his own house band for many years.

This was 1961 and Majorca was so inexpensive that I had moved into a five-roomed apartment, an elderly Spanish lady did all my washing and cleaning, with rent for £3, yes £3, per week. I was twenty-one and the world was my oyster, until the lurgy struck and I got some parasite living in my intestines. We were always told not to drink the water and with Bacardi rum at only 5s a bottle, we resolved never to touch the stuff. A typical day was spent taking a bottle of Bacardi and a pound of bananas to the beach and waiting to be recognised as one of the singers from Tito's. But this became more and more difficult as I was now seriously suffering with the squits and there were no such things as public toilets in Majorca in 1961. I could not understand where the bug had come from as the only thing that could constitute water was the ice in the Cuba Libre. It was only when I discovered where the ice was made - in large troughs with little black things scurrying around in it - did I realise what I had living in my intestines. I was losing weight and running out of strength and had to spend time stuffing lumps of cotton wool up my bum before going on stage. To cough would have been the kiss of death.

There was a small bar next to Tito's called the Monaco Bar and I had breakfast there everyday. There was a really friendly Spanish waiter called Joe and we struck up a deal: I would teach him English and he would direct the most stunning girls into my company. It worked fantastically well. I was teaching him Cockney English, ''Allo me old cock sparrow, duck and dive,' and he was introducing me to Swedish Britt Ekland lookalikes. The Plaza Gomilla was my playground and was only five minutes walk from my house so there was much traffic to and fro. As stunning as Swedish girls were, they seemed very unemotional and their beauty soon paled for the need of some comical conversation too.

I sang most nights on my own in a jazz club close to Tito's with Phil Phillips after the show and got quite a following of my own without the rest of the group. Most nights a really handsome six foot-two, white-blonde haired guy came in. He was always immaculate and I found out he was a Canadian C.E.O. for the Miller Lite American beer company. He had a stunning girlfriend who was a German hotel heiress. Without me knowing it she became quite taken with me. While I was on stage one night, one of the waiters slipped me a note from her asking for a dinner date. I was shocked and surprised but of course agreed. Little did I know that this was to be one of the most embarrassing moments of my life. We agreed to meet in the Plaza and go to a secluded bay at Santa Ponsa, a stunning bay with olive trees on a gentle slope down to an azure sea. She arrived in a silver 350 SL Mercedes convertable and she tossed me the keys to drive. My driving record up to this time consisted of a few hours behind the wheel of an old Mini, but, so as not to appear too unwordly in her formidable company, I nonchalently caught the keys and slipped into the driver's seat. I did not have a clue how to drive such an incredible machine and especially as it was an automatic. We set off at a grand speed with me inadvertantly looking at the rev counter thinking it was the speedo. We were hairing along dust tracks passing donkey carts at breakneck speed and we reached the bay in double quick time and both alighted from the car - me wondering if she had noticed I had not a clue at what we had just been through and her looking at me as though I was some kind of speed freak. I parked the car and she told me her maid had put a hamper in the boot. I laid a blanket on the ground and unloaded the hamper which contained a bottle of Cristal champagne, foie gras, caviar and an abundance of other really expensive food and drink. Appearing on stage in such salubrious settings looks really glamourous but actually it doesn't guarantee that what you are being paid is anywhere near how attractive it looks. In fact, the reverse is usually the case and the artists are scratching about for a living hoping they won't be found out. So this level of opulence made me feel ill at ease, though I need not have worried because this pampered heiress was most taken with my devil-may-care attitude and athleticism. We swam, we ate and drank and we petted all day.

One of the things that changes if you spend any time in the sun is your sleeping routine. In the beginning you are up at the crack of dawn to get to the beach and soak up the rays. But after more than a year in the rays, my sleeping habits and the amount of time spent in bed had turned topsy turvy: I was now going out all night and getting to bed around 7 a.m. and getting up around 1 p.m., so what with the parasite still living in my intestines, the many sexual gymnastics and the lack of sleep, I had taken the precaution of asking Colin for a couple of Dexadrine amphetamine tabs to keep me awake for this

74

date. What a mistake that would turn out to be. True, the pills kept me on top form all day. I declined the drive back and admired the lady's expertise and total air of confidence. As we pulled into her villa, we were greeted by her maid who told us baths would be run and dinner was set for 7 p.m. I felt eager and expectant at what the evening would bring and there was electricity in the air as we both came dressed to a long wooden table and took a seat at each end, glancing at each other over the candles and an array of wonderful food. We ate, drank and laughed, and the air was full of sexual expectancy. Then we finally made our way to a candle-lit, perfumed bedroom, disrobed each other and lay naked on the bed. One thing I had not taken into account was the fact that, though I was wide awake and highly aroused, it would not show in the old John Thomas department. The old chap had never let me down and now here I was in the most fantastic setting and the blasted pills had wiped out any erectile activity at all. I did all I could to get the old chap to work: frequent visits to the bathroom and pounding on it ferociously, whispering and cursing at it to no avail. What experience I had gained in such a dilemma was that if one becomes unable in the hips you become adroight in the lips. I could feel that my heiress was disappointed and dismayed so she fell asleep I crept away with my old J.T. in disgrace. Next time at the the club she came in and made a tosser gesture and my embarassment was complete.

The season was coming to an end, we had been really sucessful but you are only as good as your next gig. We had made friends with many European tour guides in the hope of them getting us bookings all over Europe. One contact really paid off and we arranged a week's work in a jazz club in Oslo. The problem was getting there. We only had enough money to fly to Barcelona and then to book a train ride from Barcelona to Oslo. This entailed a journey of about four days, passing through many frontiers. Freedom of movement in 1961 was not as simple as it is now and border controls were very strict. We arrived at Barcelona train station and asked for four tickets to Oslo. Now Spain in the sixties was a very *manyana* country and there was a flurry of activity to arrange such an unusual request. With much ado and several hours of waiting, we were handed a wad of tickets that was about three inches thick. We boarded the first train that would get us out of Spain. As we trundled through Spain on the type of train you would find in a Spaghetti Western, we totted up how much money we had. Unfortunately it was all in pesetas and we would have to go through France, Belgium, Holland and Denmark before we arrived in Oslo.

8. It's a long way to Oslo!

The first main stop was in Paris to change trains. We were starving by now and Paris was very expensive so we changed what little money we had into Francs and headed for an inexpensive bar near the station. We put all the money in a kitty and tossed up for who was going to eat. Two of the four were sent in to order some food that could fill a hole in their tummy but would also be easily transportable in filled overcoat pockets. This consisted of as much bread as it was possible to purloin and pots of jam and pate and butter. The two guys came out with their pockets bulging chased by fierce, hostile looks from the barman whose counter had been cleared of all the snacks when his back was turned.

With 'There's No Business Like Showbusiness' ringing in our ears, we got on and off numerous trains and became more and more dishevelled, unkempt and starving hungry. We really eked out our stash of bread and ate it with fluff and jam on it. Borders came and went and we arrived at the ferry to take us to Oslo. After a wash and brush up we decided to do an impromptu show in one of the ship's lounges and, between exhaustion through lack of food and the rolling of the ship, we delivered a selection of our best unaccompanied songs. It was a resounding success and we were not too proud to take the hat around and we raised enough money for the first decent meal we had had in days.

We arrived in Oslo to be greeted by a small fan club made up of

Norwegians who had been to Majorca that summer. It was they who had fixed up the gig at the jazz club even though, strictly speaking, we were a harmony group and not a straight heavy jazz group. Included in our repetoire were some show songs and even some comedy bits too. We were set up in Norwegian's houses and they were the most hospitable people I had ever met. Nothing was too much trouble and everything was accompanied by a shot of schnapps, they called it *yem brew* which, when translated into English, meant 'made at home 90% proof guaranteed to knock your socks off'.

We were amazed and delighted to find that we were following *Stan Getz*, an incredible saxophonist, and preceeding *George Shearing* and *Louis Armstrong*. Rehearsals went fantastically well. The musicians were the best and they liked our light-hearted numbers. Opening night was a blast and we ran out of encores. During the week we asked the proprietor how we were going and he told us that we had upped the membership by almost three hundred more patrons, most of them female. We were roaring!

After the gig we relaxed with the clientele and found that the guys' main object was to get blind drunk, which meant there was very little time being spent on the surfeit of stunning women. There were no petty jealousies as we would have experienced in England, everyone was just having a good time. Some of the best sport was to ask Norwegians about their neighbours, the Swedes. Many mimed attempts at hanging and suicide was played out. The Norwegians said that all the Scandinavians were terrible alcoholics because of the long winters and the tax on alcohol, but all in all they considered themselves the only one of the group to have a big sense of humour.

We finished the gig in Oslo and we were booked to go to Stockholm in Sweden. We had to do what they call a showcase, that's to say, a show in front of all the clubs and municipal parks as part of the government's programme of free shows in the summer. We got top rating and years later we were amazed to see that we had got more bookings than the then almost-unheard-of *Beatles* and *Cliff Richard!* These gigs would start off in an orderly and attentive fashion and then progress into minor bouts of mayhem. We thought it was something to do with us but we were happy to find out that it was due to the Swedish equivalent of *yem brew*. There was alcohol rationing in Sweden in the sixties so most people went out with hip flasks filled with this 90% proof firewater. Clubs and other venues had security people going around smelling the bottles of cola that the patrons would be swigging from, and, after a time, we would see the same security people with their hats slightly askew just tottering about, having smelt the cola bottle and taking a swig they would find it had been topped up with the *yem brew*. They and the assembled crowd would be off their heads in no time.

Sweden was first class. The people were stunningly attractive and intelligent but they lacked the humour of the Norwegians and definitely the English. The Swedes, Norwegians and Danes were likened to the English, Scottish and the Welsh in that they are all very similar but differing in their seriousness and humour.

79

9. Back to the UK & Show Time

We had been seen by some British agents in the Swedish auditions and they wrote asking us to come to see them when we got back to England. We finished all our contracts and we made moves to get back home. We had lots of meetings with different agents before signing with an agency called *Forrester George* who had offices in Park Lane, London. They were the agents for many of the biggest names in showbiz, chiefly *Ken Dodd,* who was huge in the sixties, along with *Mike Yarwood* and many more. Forrester was a typical agent: he always had a large cigar on the go, big horn-rimmed glasses and spoke in a slow Jewish drawl. We signed up with the agency for five years, shook hands and waited for the first booking to come in. We didn't have to wait long and the first call was for *George and Alfred Black's* Easter show in Coventry. George and Alfred Black were the top spring, summer and winter theatre show producers in Great Britain and to be accepted by them meant filling the books for large chunks of the year. The show in Coventry was the top show in England at Easter. The cast was headlined by the then great *Dickie Henderson*, up and coming *Jimmy Tarbuck,* the dimimutive *Jimmy Clitheroe, Susan Lane, Pinky and Perky,* jugglers, acrobats, thirty dancers and a huge orchestra.

Part of our appeal to managements was that we were able as a group to sing and dance and help out in sketches and they proceeded to get their money's worth from us. The season went really well and we got on with everyone. To keep shows alive, we played lots of pranks to fill the time when we were not on stage. One such prank was to tell the lady singer, who was quite a nervous but incredible lady, that her tannoy must be broken as she seemed to have missed her cue for one of the show's big production numbers. We would watch her rushing at a hundred miles an hour to get on stage only to be told we had pulled a stunt on her. She and her husband would think of ways to get their own back on us but without success, until one show they insisted our tannoy was not working and that we had been called. What an old ruse, we thought and we took no notice. John our dodgy bass singer wandered off to watch the show from the side of the stage. We were lolling in the dressing room when someone came in and turned on our tannoy and we were greeted by a thirtypiece orchestra and a not-too-good bass voice singing his harmony line badly to *The Easter Parade'*, surrounded by all the dancers and not having the presence of mind to sing the melody. It was awful and we were chastised by the management and it never happened again.

We finished the show at Coventry on a high and were commended by the management and Forrester George were very pleased with us. We had a whole string of club dates lined up all over the country. In the sixties in Manchester alone there were over three hundred sporting clubs, workingmen's clubs and nightclubs to play. A typical night's work would have us kick off a show at, say, The Southern Sporting Club, where there would be a whole evening's entertainment from top comics, jugglers and even wrestling. Sometimes we would have to do the first show at 8 p.m. singing in the wrestling ring. We would finish our spot there and go to the other side of Manchester to do a show in a workingmen's club. We would finish that show and do a late-night show at one of the top nightclubs in the centre of Manchester or The Whisky-a-GoGo at Cheetham Hill. We were so busy working, our feet never touched the ground.

I consider myself to be very fortunate with the life I have been given, but think that God's plan for me was to be a hard-won set of trials. I got almost to the top of everything I applied myself to, but the last, great step to complete success always just eluded me or slipped away. It has happened so many times for me to know it is not just bad luck but some higher plan to keep me fretting and fighting. Timing seems to be all in the equation of success and no matter what you do personally time and tide has an agenda of its own that you have no control over. One such incident occurred at The Whisky-a-GoGo. We were booked to do the late-night show in the nightclub casino. I learned in later years that the girl singer in the house band was *Elkie Brookes* who went on to be a big recording artist. The booking also meant that we had to do a show upstairs in the ballroom to a very young audience of pop lovers. We were not a pop act so we put together a selection of songs that might appeal to a much younger crowd than we were used to working to. The young group that was playing the ballroom had to do our spot in the nightclub on this one night of a week's booking. We didn't exactly tear up the spot we did but we went down alright with some Drifters and Motown songs. On the other hand, the young group that did our spot died the death. But, as I said before, fate and timing are very strange powers in the chance of life. That group went on to be Herman and the Hermits, having huge recording success and we carried on in showbusiness.

We pleaded with Forrester George to get us a record deal. Showbusiness was not run by the recording business - they were two very separate entities. Very few artists' careers were created by recording hit songs. Firstly you had to learn your trade and only when you had acquired all the stage craft, would you be given a recording contract to reach a much bigger audience. We got ourselves a record deal with *Decca Records* and we went into the studio to make our first record. We did a version of a *Righteous Brothers* song and it was very well accepted by the record company and our own management. Then time and fate stepped in again and lo and behold The Beatles brought out a record that was to completely change the face of showbusiness forever. Our recording company was run by an old school of showbusiness names and faces and, after feeling the shock of the phenomena that was *The Beatles*, they went on to change their recording policy and dropped most of their artists to concentrate on the new sounds coming out of youth groups all over the country. Our recording career was short and sweet, so we were back on the road.

We were accepted as a very good strong act and we never stopped working in clubs all over the country. There were so many places to play and we were having a great time but without a successful record, bookings became harder and harder to get. We had sowed our wild oats all over Britain and Europe and now two of the guys wanted to get married. Money became a more important commodity than just having a good time and things were becoming rather stressed with our agency. Agents by their nature are willing to work for an act that almost books itself so that even if you are not top of the bill you have a useful place in an agency's affairs as a solid, value-for-money act. There are innumerable accounts in books and films of the conniving ways of the middle man. He demands one price for his product and fights to get you to accept his proposal for a great booking, a great career move, prove the point to a new management this time and steam in for double the fee when you have proved how great you are. You find that you spend more time proving how great you are when you are eager, young and naive but as you get older in the tooth you recognise all the ploys and you have the mistaken belief that your agent is working for you. If you didn't work solidly from September to New Year's Day having done a summer season, then the beginning of the New Year would be very bleak financially. Without a record deal, there was no constant source of free publicity on radio and TV. This had become so important and many acts that had been successful for many years were feeling the pinch, ourselves included. This one particular year, we had finished the Christmas dates and New Year, and then the telephone stayed silent for what seemed an eternity. Our constant entreaties to our agents bore no bookings at all. We had to do something or we were worried we might have to get a real job. Ouch!

Our agent spoke so slowly on the telephone that we could hardly afford to call him and the pips on the machine meant we almost always ran out of money before we were given any news. We all made a trip up to London to the office where we were greeted warmly and sat to be told that the business was in turmoil and bookings for acts like ours were down. One glimmer of hope was a summer show in Blackpool which was due to start in the first week in June. But this was only March and, even though it was to be a long booking from rehearsals in the last week in May to the final show in the last week in September, it was a long wait to start work. We were elated at the news before the bomb dropped. Things had been tough, the agent told us and there had not been many requests for our services. He advised us to accept this booking to give us all time to concentrate on where our plans would take us next, whilst we had money coming in. We all agreed that this was a sensible decision and then we asked the $64 million question: how much would the job pay? Without blinking an eye, and knowing full well the financial hole we were, in he said £160 a week, net. We assumed that was £160 each but he said that, no this was for the group. We had been on from £300 to £500 a week for the act and now we were being offered this paltry sum. We left the office knowing there was no other offer in sight and nothing else in the book to look forward to. We went to have a drink to discuss what we should do. The married guys, Colin and John, agreed that the agent must be taking the piss. Myself and Mac absolutely refused to work for so little money. This felt as though it could be the end of the group. We went home and the weeks went by before we finally agreed to accept the booking at this price, just this one time and then we would look for another agent.

May came around. We had not seen each other for a couple of months, as we had not had the money to get together to rehearse. We met at the Central Pier in Blackpool for our first show. It was not one of the best gigs but we had bitten the bullet and were determined, as always, to do the best show it was possible to do irrespective of the little money we were being paid. We moved into a dressing room and looked

Blackpool

for somebody to tell us what we had to do and were greeted by a very nice man who asked us who we were. 'The Gale Boys,' came our reply.

'What are you doing here, lads? You're on at The Grand in The Arthur Haynes Show.'

This bombshell hit us like a ton of bricks: we had signed away a whole summer season at the second best show in town for £40 each a week doing our own spot and working in all the musical production numbers and helping in sketches with Arthur Haynes too. With the strains of *'There's No Business Like Showbusiness'* ringing in our ears again, we spent the summer starving.

The show was a fantastic success. It was a great team which

included Nicholas Parsons, Dermott Kelly and Rita Webb. Arthur Haynes loved our professionalism and said he wanted us to work with him again as he had some more shows and a television series coming up. Armed with this information, we knew we had bargaining points for the money we wanted next time. We had truly served our apprenticeship even after all the things we had been through and we wanted our money's worth.

Blackpool had been a great season and we had managed to get our date book filled for the rest of the year and the beginning of the next. Blackpool had all the great acts in for the season and our main rivals were The Batchelors and The Seekers. Ken Dodd was the biggest draw in Blackpool and he heard how well we had gone down. He wanted to use us on his television show and this proved to be another great success and the dates came flooding in.

One of the great driving forces of the business is that one day you can be on your uppers and the next day your head is in the clouds.

10. The Lure of Spain

The summer finished and we extended it by getting some more bookings in Spain. The money was good and the cost of living made your wages worth four times as much. We did a month's work in a new resort on the coast called Benidorm, in a club called *El Burros*, The Donkeys. It was a really nice restaurant with baby donkeys walking around whilst you ate. Benidorm was brand new and the resort had only just started to grow. We had a great time and were invited up to an American radar station in the mountains in a town called Alcoy, to spend some time when we had finished at *El Burros*, to do some shows and live with some of the families who manned the base.

We moved into American service families' homes and were a source of amusement to them with our accents. Not many of them had spent any time with English people and I thrilled my host's wife by accepting a drink of iced tea, something I had never had time to ask for in England as we drank tea to warm us up. 'My mother will never believe that I served iced tea to a Englishman for the first time!' She was made up.

Beau was a Master Sergeant who had been through the Second World War and Korea. He had great respect for the English forces and told interesting stories about the war. He said the toughest troops were the Turks, especially if they were captured, and that the American forces would not go anywhere without a tank and a wagon full of ice-cream and cola in front of them. Beau was an all-American boy, a real Robert Redford lookalike. He had a close-knit family: a beautiful wife and two sons, one of fourteen and another of fifteen. They were built like the proverbial brick out-houses, big and strong enough to be American football quarterbacks. We sat down each morning to a feast of eggs sunny-side up or light over easy, (we thought you just fried them!), Canadian streaky bacon grits (another new experience that tasted like fried semolina), copious amounts of toast, orange juice and coffee. The adults would be seated at the table and two large figures would appear at the end of the table, stiff, straight-backed: 'Good morning. Orders for the day, sir.' Beau gave them their chores for the day and they said, 'Sir, yes, Sir,' and left to complete them. I was so impressed by their respect so I asked Beau how he was able to command so much humility without having to resort to the fact that he was a Master Sergeant. 'We have an arrangement,' he said. 'When they have finished their chores, they look forward to challenging me to any number of sports that day, running, tennis, swimming – anything – and the day they beat me, they need not refer to me as "Sir" again.' The result seemed so successful that I employed it later in my own life when I had a family of my own, although I could never make it work on my wife. The love and respect I felt in that family was something I had never seen before. I congratulated Beau and he said, the way things were going, he would not be hearing that word for very much longer as the boys were on a mission.

We said goodbye to the families with a big show we put on for the colonel, who gave us the pleasure of a trip around an American PX. This is a shop on the base stocked with everything an American serviceman could hope for, anything from a needle to an order for a Cadillac. We were not allowed to purchase anything for ourselves but some things were purchased by proxy.

The next stop on our tour was a short season at a restaurant nightclub in Madrid. The Parillia Rex was a top club frequented by all the top Spanish matadors including the charismatic figure of El Cordobez, the top man in Spanish bull fighting at the time. He and the other matadors would be accompanied by film stars, models and the *crème de la crème* of feminine beauties. The floor show was extravagant and the dancers were the pick of the top dancers in Europe - tall, stunning, long-legged beauties. We thought we had died and gone to heaven. Every night after the show, tall, dark-skinned Latin lotharios would be waiting for the girls to finish the show. We chided them for their greased back hair and the fact that they had suits with sleeves in them, but they never put them on, they just draped them on their shoulders. The girls loved our sense of humour, commiserating with them for their broken arms. What we found throughout our professional career was that the stunning dancers who have been romanced by the top lotharios, soon tired of them and searched for guys with a sense of humour. That's where we came in.

After Madrid, we moved on to a short season in Barcelona at a nightclub called the Emporium on Las Ramblas, the main thoroughfare in Barcelona. This was an earthy, intruiging place, full of hostesses and real characters. Once again, the show was lavish and exciting.

11. Who'd Wanna be a Star?

There is only so much appreciation that is of any value from your fellow artists and peers so all the respect for your good name and professionalism can help to keep you working. It is your value as a financial draw to a booking management that can keep the bookings coming in. No matter how big the management they don't like to have to work too hard to sell their acts: they like bookers to enquire about your availability then they can talk money. But you have to be a draw and that means publicity through recordings and television appearances. We had neither of these as well-known as we were in the business, so without this guarantee of drawing a crowd we were destined to spend our life on the road. The business was rapidly changing, venues were closing down due to the new musical phenomena that were The Beatles and The Rolling Stones and all the other young groups.

We arrived back in England and went straight into rehearsals for a summer show in Bournemouth, one of the best seasons in the country. We were joining *The Russ Conway Show* at The Winter Garden. This was not a proper theatre but a huge orchestral auditorium and it was a wide open expanse with no tabs *(curtains)*. Russ Conway was a huge draw and he was the English equivalent of Liberace, though perhaps not as flamboyant as his American counterpart. The season was being shared on a monthly change over of top female singers, kicking off with Dusty Springfield, then Cleo Laine, Adele Leigh and finally

Dorothy Squires.

We were treated to a most hilairious 'who's best' (that's the walk down at the end of the show when you can guage by your applause how much the audience liked your performance). One night, Russ Conway paged Dorothy Squires for her walk down and, as the words 'The inimitable Miss Squires' left Russ Conway's lips, Dorothy staggered onto the stage swearing all kinds of love for all and sundry and proceeded to take Russ in a bear hug and dance around the stage for an interminable amount of time. The orchestra and cast were at a loss for what to do so the orchestra kept playing as Dorothy hugged and danced with Russ. There were no curtains to ring down and no hook long enough to tear the two stars off the stage so one of Miss Squires' entourage was summoned to extract the pair as delicately and subtly as possible. Dorothy wouldn't let go of Russ and the pair exited the stage to shouts of *bravo* from the audience. During the run of the show in Bournemouth we would jump into our trusty mini minor after the show on a Saturday night and rush up to Blackpool to do a Sunday concert with other big stars like Ken Dodd. Now this was before motorways and it was all A and B roads, and in the wee small hours of the morning it used to take about six hours to get there. We would peel ourselves out of a fart-laden mini and prepare to do a band-call at the Opera house,the Grand or the ABC theatres. We were knackered but the old trouper spirit always kicked in. Life on the road was exhausting but full of laughs and I was in showbiz.

The other theatre in Bournemouth was The Pavillion and the star of the show was our old friend Arthur Haynes. He was supported by The Seekers headed by Judith Durham who was responsible for their very distinctive sound. We envied their recording career and the wealth and fortune that came with it, as they drove around in brand new XK140 Jaguars and we had a group Mini Minor. We got a most welcome call one day: Judith had come down with a serious throat infection and without her the group were unable to perform. Unlike us they were strictly a recording group and as such were very static on stage and were not able to join in with the rest of Arthur's show. Our management were asked if we could fill in their spot until she got better. Timings were worked out and we rushed from our show every day to fill The Seekers' spot until Judith improved. Tiring as this was, we were only too delighted to work with Arthur Haynes again. Arthur enjoyed us so much he said he would like to use us in his next television series. He said he would be off after the summer show to make a film in Hollywood with Rock Hudson. That would take about four months and then he went straight into rehearsals for the television series. We were so pleased and our management said it was just the exposure we needed to work on creating music for a much needed recording career. But, like many things in my career, it wasn't to be. Arthur went to Hollywood and had a heart attack and died. Poor man, poor us.

12. Dark Days

This was the start of a dark time in my life. I was still only twenty-five and single and had only the responsibilty of looking after myself so it should have been the time of my life. But, after much heartache and suffering by my lovely dad, he passed away. My father's death hit me hard because it meant that my dear mother was on her own. I had to work away from home to make a living and, although my skuldugerous brother was still at home, it was not easy to rely on him. Now I had other things to worry about apart from myself. Added to this, my poor mother had a stroke and was almost unable to look after herself. Life was getting tougher. But there was light in those dark times. During the summer season I had met the most beautiful Doris Day lookalike and she became the love of my life and would later become my wife.

Because of ever greater commitments and a rapidly changing business, finances were playing an ever greater threat to our dedication to the act. Cracks began to show between ourselves and our management. The gigs began to slow down and we were spending longer and longer apart. When we were single, without the intrusion of wives and lovers, it was easy to dedicate ourselves to the act - it always came first. But people who were not in the act had issues of their own to consider. We had always said that anything that would come between our dedication to the act was paramount because that constituted who and what we were. So during the seven years that we were together, love was not allowed to interfere with the act. When it looked as though any woman was getting too close to any member, we pulled the most awful strokes on each other to break up erstwhile romances, to the point of laying down a law that girls had to be shared or at least spied on. We were young and full of fun so any liaison had to have an element of laughter attached to it. We created a watchers club to be able to spy on any sexual activity. If one or more of the group pulled a girl, arrangements were made back at the hotel to get the bed lined up with the key-hole so that whoever was not in the room was able to see the gymnastics on the bed. To do this you had to have your watchers outfit on. This consisted of a see-through mac, a flat cap and the top off a Watney's bottle. Adorned in this and stark naked beneath the mac with the Watney's top mounted on the lapel of the mac we paraded though hotel corridors all over the country in the early hours of the morning. We would invariably be drunk and stiffling guffaws of laughter while trying to look through the key-hole at what was happening on the bed in the room. Trying to subdue laughter in the wee small hours of the morning was so much more interesting and liberating than taking sex with anybody very seriously. Hence we were able to ward off any romances or intrusions to our main preoccupation in life, becoming a really successful group.

1966 in England was the greatest place to be in the world. The country was positive, vibrant and exciting. We had just won the World Cup, The Beatles, The Stones, The Who and hundreds of different groups were taking over the musical world. The economy was booming and the country was awash with money. There were so many nightclubs and workingmen's clubs putting on entertainment that our date book was full. We were earning good money and just intent on keeping going. Manchester, Newcastle, Leeds, Birmingham were bursting at the seams with entertainment. Take for instance a place like Doncaster, there was a club called *The Scala*. Now even a workingman's club like this on a Sunday afternoon would have six different acts on. Top of the bill when we worked it was Matt Monroe who was at the top of the charts at the time. On the bill with him was Susan Maugham and comic Norman Collier, ourselves and a ventriloquist and a magician. The booze was subsidised by the brewery and the club was run by a commitee of ordinary working men, mainly coal miners, who, though they were down-to-earth Yorkshiremen, had a huge budget to pay for this much entertainment. One night, just after the show, we were standing at the bar with Matt Monroe when the club secretary asked if he could pay us. The thing that artists hate the most is for other acts to find out how much they were being paid. Matt Monroe's chin fell to the ground as the club secretary began counting out to Matt's outstretched hand, ten, twenty, thirty, forty and so on with Matt trying to stop him and the secretary commenting to all and sundry, 'I'd have to work a year to take home a fraction of this kind of wages.' By this time all the artists were thanking God that he hadn't chosen them to start and the club secretary was unaware of the embarassment he was causing this big star.

Being young and fancy-free we thought this could go on forever; we had a great act and we lived right up to our means. Now responsibility was cutting in and the first cracks began to show as the bookings began to slow down and we had made no provisions to save. The three guys were married now and each wife was making noises about their need for financial security. It soon became a source of discontent. One day, John the bass singer said he and his wife had been offered a job outside of showbusiness and they could not afford not to take it. We agreed to John leaving which would help our performance and certainly mean more money, although the agency said we were no longer The Gale Boys people knew and our fees may be affected accordingly. We totally ignored this knowing it was yet another ploy to take more money before it was paid to us. John left and it didn't affect the working of the group at all except that Colin who usually bunked down with John was now left to his own resources which was not ideal. He was enormously engaging, funny and talented. But he was living proof of the saying that God had endowed men with a penis and a brain but not enough blood to work the two of them at the same time. Colin had an abundance of talent but zero self control and, what with his dependence on dexatrine to keep his weight down, his exuberance and love of life got completely out of control. One week we finished a huge nightclub date in Birmingham; we'd had a great week and the management loved us. But when we went to get paid we were told by the club accountant that Colin had already drawn a large amount of what we were owed and as it transpired had spent it in the casino of the club. Fierce argument and recrimination ensued and we went home with not a lot of money to keep us going till our next gig.

13. **Jon Jon is Born**

I was sharing my time between my mother's house in Dagenham and my girlfriend's house in Bournemouth. There was not a lot of money coming in and we had no work in the book for another month. I received a letter from Mac telling me his wife was pregnant and he could not rely on the bookings we had to supply the needs for a new baby. The letter said that, with great regret after all we had been through, he was resigning from the group. I totally understood his concerns but was devastated at what the future now held for me. With very little money saved, my girlfriend and I decided to move in together. There was little work to be had in Bournemouth after the summer season and she had been offered a place to live in Buckinghamshire. We moved to a casino called *The Woburn Grange Country Club,* run by a friend of my girlfriend and owned by a Corsican casino expert. The club turned out to be the place they used for the opening shots for *Fawlty Towers* in the famous John Cleese television series.

My girlfriend worked as a croupier and I helped to rebuild and maintain the club. This opened a whole new chapter in my life. No longer in showbusiness, I became quite depressed at the prospect at being an odd job man. Casino life seems very romantic but it was real tough. Sometimes we would stay open for as long as the punters wanted to play. Having finished my work, I would help out in the bar with an Italian man called Eugene who was an affable, congenial bloke, a perfect barman able to share the delights of the punters when they won, and commiserate with them when they lost. He taught me how to get a bigger tip from the gamblers at the tables. He would take a tray, pour a little water in it and load up the customers' order. I asked him why the water in the tray and he told me to follow him. I watched as he delivered the drink to the gambler at the table. Gamblers are always transfixed by the spinning wheel and will put on chips right up until the moment the ball drops. There was a flurry as the number was called and Eugene placed the

Transfixed by the spinning wheel

drink on the side table next to the gambler. The gambler put a large denomination chip on the tray, still concentrating on the wheel. Eugene changed the large chip for smaller ones as change and, timing it as the next spin of the wheel was called, the punter scrabbled to take what was a small amount of chips compared to what he was gambling, Eugene would just tilt the tray to have what chips were left slide on the water to his side of the tray. '*Merci monsieur*.' This ploy never failed and Eugene went on to open his own restaurant with the proceeds.

I made a decision to ask the Corsican, a really tough man, if I could train to be a croupier. He said he thought I would never ask and so I started training straight away. I could deal Black Jack, Roulette and other games and started a journey into a totally different way of life. Before I had spent my life trying to cheer people up, now I was sitting at a table for hours on end dealing to people's insatiable urge to beat the bank and watching them win one moment and be elated, then lose and become totally depressed. It was a whole new ballgame for me. I spent two years working as a croupier and during that time my girlfriend and I had our first baby. I can honestly say that the shoes I wore to work in the casino never trod on anything that was not carpeted for two years.

The work as a croupier was intense and very stressful; you had to concentrate all the time. My girlfriend and I were saving like mad and we were determined to get a deposit for a house. All the time, I was yearning to get back into what I enjoyed doing most, trying to cheer people up through music and laughter.

Woburn Grange was only an hour's drive from London down the M4 and I started buying the showbusiness trade papers again. Rock and pop had really taken over the scene by then but I had no experience in that field so I had to stick to what I knew - live entertainment. I got an audition to be the lead singer in a big club called The Showboat on the Strand just off Trafalgar Square. I passed the audition and started working for a real taskmaster called Jack Fallon. He would get you doubling up on all things to run the club as well as appearing in the show. He was responsible for giving stars like Dave Allen their first big gig in London. The production lasted for six months and I shared the bill with some up and coming stars. I was signed up for a year and felt I was able to move out of the club and buy a flat. My girlfriend was pregnant again and she swore she would not have the baby at the club. She was, and remains, the sole driving force of whatever I have been able to achieve; having set her mind on a goal, she would not let either of us rest until the goal had been accomplished. With this determination we moved into a brand-new apartment and finished putting the last touches to a brand-new bed. At 3 a..m., as we lay down exhausted to sleep, I had no sooner closed my eyes when she nudged me and told me the baby was coming. She had lived up to her word and I rushed her to the hospital where my son was born.

With a mortgage and two babies, it was not possible to live on the salary of one club, so I found myself having to double or even treble my appearances at clubs all over the capital. On top of that, I spent Sundays fitting in a workingman's club out of town. I finished the year in London and got some solo bookings on the recomendation of some of the acts I had worked with and then went off to appear around the club circuit in England and Scotland. Far from being glamorous, it was lonely and unedifying. When I was in the group, I often yearned to be a solo entertainer thinking the financial rewards and the acclaim must be much sweeter on your own. But the truth was far from the dream; as soon as the applause died down, the reality of living in damp digs in Leeds or Middlesborough alone and far from home kicked in. I spent twenty-three lonely, miserable hours for every one hour of fame on stage. From England, I moved on to Scotland. It was terryfying! Scotland was the only place that a club booker threatened not to pay me. One night, after playing my heart out, the booker told me that my performance was not up to scratch. Angry, I argued it was because his backing band were unable to read my music, saying they only knew music with a picture on the front. The mere fact that some of my arrangements were written by Peter Knight who had written for people like Sammy Davis Jnr. held no sway. I eventually got my money under some duress and went to the nearest shop to buy some music with pictures on the front. An Englishman alone in a Scottish workingman's club is an absolute fool, a brave man or incredibly naive. I suppose I was naïve; what a fool. Some of the bookings were totally crazy. I was booked as part of the cabaret for a big Scottish football club and the backing for my act was bagpipes, drums and sax. It was mayhem. No amount of pleading on my part could get them to see that 'The Lady is a Tramp' was not best played on the bagpipes. In fact, they thought that it was an affront for some Sassenach to even question Big Willie's ability to play anything at all on this sacred instrument. One other night I was booked to do a show on a Sunday afternoon at the Tillybuddy workingman's club. The commitee was nice, the band just OK. I changed into a white jacket, black trousers and shirt to do the show. I was standing waiting to go on when a guy said, 'Are you the turn?'

'Yes,' I replied.

He asked me what my show consisted of and I told him that I did songs and some impressions. To which he replied that he thought I seemed like an awful nice man and that the stains of blood on a white jacket was not a sight he wished to behold, 'Do yourself a favour old chap, put your jeans on and sing some Rock & Roll for God's sake.'

I couldn't change my programme at the last minute and so I went on and, as predicted, died. The rest of my tour around Scotland was pretty much as bad; I contracted a serious throat infection and was miserable as sin.

One night I was finishing up the last date I had in Glasgow. By this point, for safety's sake, I had acquired a near-perfect Scottish accent. I went into a pub in Glasgow and ordered a light and bitter as a night cap before going to bed and escaping across the border the next day. My accent must have slipped as, before the last syllable had left my lips, the bar went quiet and the barman backed away from me. The hackles on my neck stood up as I expected violence to rain down upon me and a split second passed as the rumble of Scotsmen about to do damage to a Sassenach was interrupted by a loud Cockney voice that rang out, 'Steady lads. This guy must be plain stupid or monumentally brave. I think the first of those two options is the case and besides I happen to know him so back off please.' My saviour was none other than the incredible Wee Willy Harris, loved and revered by all who loved Rock & Roll. I was saved. I spent the night in a drunken stupor thinking how lucky I had been. I never left London to entertain again.

14. Maidenhead to *'Talk of the Town'*

My darling partner and I had three children now. The apartment was too small and we decided to look for a house to renovate. We chose Maidenhead and we found an old run-down cottage that needed completely gutting and

rebuilding. It only had two rooms upstairs and a tiny kitchen and toilet downstairs - it had been a coachman's cottage to a big house next door We bought the cottage for £5,000 in 1971 and started work on it straightaway. The dust and rubble was unbearable

Our run-down cottage

with three small children to cope with so we hired a caravan, parked it in the drive and lived in cramped but dust-free accommodation.

The cottage after renovation

I really needed to earn some money now what with the new mortgage, children and now cats too. I went for an audition at The Talk of the Town, the top live cabaret restaurant

in the whole of the United Kingdom. Hundreds of male singers went

106

for the role of lead vocalist in an extravaganza that cost £100,000 to produce. There was a thirty-six piece Burt Rhodes Orchestra, thirty dancers, a speciality act, some girl singers and a male vocalist. After three nail-biting auditions, I was offered the job. Up until now I had been working under my own name, Brian Kearney. But a guy who did similar stuff to me had changed his name from Gerry Dorsey to Englebert Humperdinck and so I decided to change my name to something silly too. So, I became Jon Jon Keefe. This was the name of a boy I had gone to school with and it seemed catchy and memorable and lucky. Here comes Jon Jon, I thought.

The producer of The Talk of the Town show was the highly respected and acclaimed Robert Nesbit. He was called the Prince of Darkness in the trade due to his incredible ability to light a show like no-one else. He was responsible for producing The Royal Command Performances at The Palladium. The choreographer was a volatile, short-tempered, gay Canadian called Billie Petch who worked with his assistant Bobbie. I felt the brunt of his caustic voice when he brought all the dancers and orchestra to a screaming halt as I walked on, stage front and centre to be featured singing 'Ma Cherie Amour'. 'Stop! Stop! Mr Keefe, you and only you are the presenter of my wonderful show and yet you walk on stage like a fucking dustman. I implore you take the opportunity to realise how many singers we turned down to give you the chance to shine, so go back again we will start the whole orchestra and the rest of the cast and technicians again so that you may walk onto my stage and look like you know what-the-fuck you are doing and how important you are to me.' It only needed one such humiliating dressing down to make me realise I never wanted to be admonished in such a way again.

The foibles of showbusiness are that though I was signed as the only male singer in this incredible show, for some reason known only to Mr Nesbitt, he saw a singer at a golf club and signed him up to share the lead with me. This reduced the impact I could have and lessened the publicity I could get for myself in the show. The singer had a light operatic voice and had hardly any experience in live performances. This was made clear when Mr Burt Rhodes came into the dressing room we shared to tell the unfortunate singer that 'Robert, it is OK to sing flat if you are able to keep it that way - I can get the musicians to help accordingly. And it's alright to sing sharp - I can get the band to deal with that as well. But if you are determined to sing flat and sharp in the song, all will be to no avail!' The singer's lack of experience and his dud musical ear meant he didn't have the ability to help with any of Mr Rhodes' requests. He was not a welcome participant of the production. Robert and I were interviewed by the showbusiness reporter of the *Daily Express* who asked us how much experience we had in the business. I told him about my journey from singing in Ronnie and Reggie's club in the East End through to playing in nightclubs, theatres and appearing on television with *The Gale Boys.* Robert's experience was a few amateur shows in Scotland, but it turned out he had been a cub football player for West Ham. I opened the newspaper to see a photo of Robert and the headline '*Ex-West Ham footballer heads £100,.000 spectacular Revue.*' It had happened again. Was God still trying to make me pay for pushing him on the back burner? I didn't know. Anyway, when the season was over, Robert married the wife of the licencee of the pub opposite The Talk's stage door and left the business.

I was house building from 9 a.m. till 5 p.m., stopping only for a bite to eat, a dip in the bath in a building site. Then I had time for thirty minutes sleep in the bath, then got up, dressed and set off to London to do the show.

The Talk of the Town was the top place in town for dinner and cabaret. During my year there I was lucky enough to see some of the

greatest names in live entertainment: my hero Sammy Davis Jnr., and Tom Jones. I also had the horrible experience of watching people throw bread rolls at Judy Garland who was obviously the worse for wear; it was so sad and humiliating.

Standing back-stage night after night and the thrill of watching a star getting a standing ovation, I did this and the star was Lovelace Watkins. I thought that live entertainment was the ability to ad-lib and make the performance as free as possible. I learned this was not the case when Lovelace came off stage to the most incredible standing ovation only to be admonished by his little Jewish manager who rebuked him for

changing a couple of words to the introduction to a song. I was amazed as he went back on to screams and cheers of the crowd. I tightened up my own performances and ceased leaving my programme to chance.

Some nights were absolutely electric. One such night belonged to the one and only Dusty Springfield. This was 1973, she had been in the States for two years and this was her first performance back in the UK. The audience was packed with showbusiness stars from both sides of the musical divide. The Beatles were in, as were The Stones, Michael Caine was there, and Sammy Davis Jnr. In fact, anybody who was anybody in showbiz or commerce was in. A ticket was a golden property and the touts were making a fortune. We finished our extravaganza, or the music to eat your soup by, as we sometimes called it, and the time had come for the top of the bill act. As I stood wing-side ready to watch the entrance of this great singer, I could feel the atmosphere in the room was electric. The band was tuning up and everyone was ready to go, when I heard a small commotion back stage – the voices of Mr Nesbitt and Michael Grade heatedly discussing who was going to go to Miss Springfield's dressing room, tell her to put on her dress and do the show. It was most unusual to see Mr Nesbitt getting flustered at all over anything, his command was carried out as part of a forgone conclusion, but alas not this time. Apparently Miss Springfield had decided to take the band-call full out and in the process had injured her voice. It was such a depressing sight to see an electrified audience let down by a non-appearance through a twist of fate. It was just horrible for all concerned.

Stories I heard from the orchestra were the bread and butter of being so close to fame. One of the guys told me that after Barbra Streisand finished a run at The Talk of the Town she gave every member of the orchestra a big box of smarties. Needless to say, that gesture went down like a lead balloon. But to add insult to injury, Billy Eckstine, who was the next big American star to come in, heard the story and, at the end of his season, did the same and gave the orchestra a box of smarties. Of course, it was accepted with smiles and *bonhomie*, but in the band room the guys thought that he was taking the piss and said so in no uncertain terms. One guy hurled his box at the wall and was followed by a succession of other guys hurling their smartie boxes. That was until one of the boxes broke open and a £20 note dropped out. The mayhem and pandamonium that ensued as the musos tried to retrieve their boxes was fantastic to behold.

Most of the singers, dancers and musicians had other gigs to do after The Talk show finished at 10.15 p.m. Getting to the next gig was always a rush and you really had to cut it fine to get there on time. One particular show was the fabulous Pearl Bailey. She was booked for a short season and, about two days into the gig, she was taken ill. She went into hospital for a check-up and someone else was booked at short notice to take her place. But Pearl signed herself out of the hospital to come back for a big charity show for the Duke of Norfolk. The management were of the opinion that it was too dangerous for Miss Bailey to do the whole show and suggested she just did about fifteen minutes to show great faith with her fans and her fighting spirit. After her opening number she declared, 'Pearl Bailey ain't gonna die in no hospital bed, Pearl Bailey is going to die doing what she does best, singing for her fans on stage.' What a trouper. Instead of her fifteen minutes, she did longer than her usual show. I stood in the wings as she held her enraptured audience in the palm of her hand eulogising about her career and her love of entertaining. But backstage, all the musicians had other gigs to get to and were now late thanks to Miss Bailey. Men kept nervously checking their watches and a sax player on the end of the orchestra, checked his watch again and mouthed, 'Please die now'.

15. Big Shows – Little Money

No-one appearing in the West End ever earned much money hence the need to do more than one show a night. If punters went to more than one club a night they were quite likely to see all the performers they had seen at the last show. Money was always tight and the best shows were well oiled by drink. There were no concessions for us to get drinks at the clubs at a reduced rate and club prices were astronomical. A Scottish bass player called Bill Sharp instigated an old touring band habit of buying your own bottle of the tipple of your choice, be it whisky or gin or whatever took your fancy, and some mixers and keeping it in a suitcase in the dressing room. If you wanted a drink you had to buy it back from the suitcase at just above pub prices. That way, at the end of the gig we had all had a great drink but we had also made a profit by charging ourselves just over the limit. That way we had money over to restock the suitcase. We figured with mathematics like that Bill should have gone on to be Chancellor of the Exchequer.

I was doing four shows a night by now and was still building our house in the daytime. As we had three children, it was decided that after all this time together maybe it was safe to get married. This we did at Maidenhead Town Hall and we asked someone who worked there to be our witness. After the ceremony, we went back to work on the house and up to London for the shows; nothing changed.

The Talk of the Town show was from 9.30 p.m. to 10.30 p.m., then

I would run up Regent Street to The L'Hirondelle for a show at 11 p.m. This was another extravaganza and this one featured myself

Jon Jon married his partner Jo

as lead vocalist, a female lead singer, about twenty leggy dancers, a soubrette and a singer and dancer called Steve Cornell. Steve was also the featured male speciality dancer at The Talk of the Town. He was as gay as it was possible to be, with a physique that any sportsman would die for.

There was not an ounce of excess fat on his body, his shoulders were as wide as a door, his whole body was in perfect proportion and he could lift a girl of ten stone over his body at arm's length whilst pirouetting at a furious pace. He had been resident at the club for many shows and considered it his home turf. He had a screamingly wicked sense of humour and that was what made us good friends. He was a magnificent example of a man and as gay as old fluffy boots. He dressed in bikers' leathers and drove a Harley Davidson.

The club, like all nightclubs in London, looked romantic and inviting at night but in the daytime was seedy and dirty. There was a glass dance floor underlit with multi coloured lights. Dance routines seemed to be a contest in trying to get as many clothed and semi-clothed bodies on as small a surface as possible. The choreographer's hair was festooned on his head like something from a Charles II portrait. He was married but it was difficult to say if he was more gay than straight. He was Scottish and spoke with a languid Scottish brogue. He was short-tempered and screamingly aggressive. The owners of the club were Turkish-Cypriots and kept a tight reign on the budget for the show. The audience consisted of a motley crew depending on the day of the week. Mid-week it would be very sparce, in a room that seated a hundred people there would be ten to thirty customers, mostly members of the aristocracy, the upper echelons or the law. Considering the amount of people in the show, the waiters and not to forget the most important people of all the hostesses, 'we called them hostages', it seemed odd that we should open for so few customers. But these customers were the principle reason the club was open at all. I once asked the Maitre D' how the club was able to make a profit in the week with so few punters and he told me that these ten or twnety people were paying £500 to £1,000 a piece. On Friday or Saturday nights, a hundred customers were paying £50 to £100 each and they were a pain.

Hostesses Disappearing Act

Watching the hostesses go to work on a punter was magical. The girls were really nice to me as I used to dedicate special songs to them. Although their punters cared not a fig for our performance, we were just a backdrop to their fumbling and groping in the dark, we knocked ourselves out singing and dancing. The girls were not prostitutes but they did make private arrangements with their punters after the show. Watching them make the customer run up a tab was brilliant. First they would put in an order from the cigarette girl with a tray around her neck colourfully and scantily dressed, 'Two hundred Marlboro please dear, then a bottle of Dom Perignon champagne for starters.' Some Peter Sellers-type waiter would decork the champagne with great flair, an elbow cocked at a ninety degree angle to his body as he poured this expensive champagne slowly and magnificently into the glass, nurturing it as it slipped gently into the glass. The hostess would reach to take a sip and invariably knock the glass over, 'Oooh look at me!' she would exclaim. 'What am I doing?' Of course, her main objective was to exhaust as many bottles as possible drinking as little of it as she could, the more the punters ordered, the higher her percentage of the profits rose. With the same flourish, the waiter would refill the glass and, as the hostess and her punter celebrated with this really expensive champagne, the waiter would surreptitiously drop his elbow to deposit a large quantity onto the carpet. Many bottles were ordered and very few of them consumed. When we left the club at night the carpets were a sodden mess.

117

The girls complained bitterly when the Boat Show, the Car Show or the Farmers' Show came to Earl's Court. The club would be heaving with raucous salesmen out for a good time on expenses celebrating the successful deals they had done. The girls really had to work hard for their money and the beady-eyed customers watched every little trick of the trade the girls tried to pull. The car dealers and the boat dealers were very much alike in their pursuit of a good time, but the farmers were a different kettle of fish altogether. The girls said some of their sexual preferences had them doing strange things with all different objects – fruits and other inanimate objects – that didn't require them to exert themselves phsically. On car dealer nights, I found that I was from the same neck of the woods as most of the punters, the only difference was that I was dressed as a South American gaucho with my arse hanging out of a pair of cowboy chaps. Steve and I opened the show standing above the stage on a plinth singing songs from the shows as the girls danced some topless in front of us. As the crowd drank more and more, they cried out, 'Look at the arse on the poofters,' amidst screams of laughter. I had no way of telling the baying crowd that I was not gay, I was not even happy, and Steve who was, took umbrage to being screamed at in this manner. We had a routine where we would come down onto the floor in our chaps armed with a bull whip which we would crack above the heads of the audience. It was choreographed but according to the amount of displeasure we felt we would inadvertantly so it seemed drop our supposedly limp wrists and give one or two of the animals a crack with the whip. Sometimes Steve would be spinning around with a girl horizontally above his head and, if he was really upset with the crowd, he would bring her down to waist height and move fractionally closer to the front row which he would proceed to demolish with her swirling, out-stretched feet. We had many ways of meting out forms of retribution as the baying wolves that were the audience unmercifully took the piss out of us. The band leader was a German saxophonist who proudly sported a black iron cross around his neck. The rest of the guys were talented, cynical Scotsmen and they were always at loggerheads. One show, the pianist, who loved a drink and smoke of pot, refused to play for any part of the show except for me. I had a spot on my own, centerstage in a pin spot and I began singing 'Maria' from *Westside Story*. With a small light on my head, I began *colle voce*, 'The most beautiful sound in the world I ever heard' when, from behind me on a small balcony, came the sound of heavy breathing and lots of noises of a sexual nature. I stopped singing and turned to the punter whose tablecloth was going up and down at an ever-increasing rate and said, 'Excuse me sir. this is my big moment in the show.' He said, 'Suit yourself but I'm paying £300 for this Wafty Crank. Let's see who can finish first.' I carried on singing and he finished first.

At the end of this show several members of the cast would rush out of the club to do another show. Steve would get on his Harley in his leathers and chains and troll around Piccadilly. I would rush off to do another show at midnight at the Le Rheims, a subterranean hole deep underground in Windmill Street, which was also owned by the owners of *The L'Hirondelle*. It was basically four girls and myself singing and dancing on a postage stamp that was called a stage. This was a real clip joint as punters were ushered off the streets of Soho downstairs to be clipped of their money. I would finish that show and rush back to The L'Hirondelle to do another show to an even more drunken rabble of a crowd.

So there I was building a house, living in a caravan and doing four shows a night, six nights a week. The money for all four shows was not good but if you went to London for one show you might as well do all you could while you were there. I was booked at The Talk of the Town for over a year and the rest of the clubs for six months at a time. It was gruelling but I would not and could not go back on the road because of the house I was building. Besides, I got as much, if not more, satisfaction from building the house as I did from performing. At least when you had finished a day's work brick laying or plastering you could step back and see the result of that day's labour. With performing you were only as good as the audience would allow you to be and even if you went down a storm, after the show the applause evaporated like a puff of smoke.

16. Out of The Blue – An Extraordinary Invitation

This now reads like a bad plot from a Hollywood movie. The Talk of the Town show really was a prestigious show to be part of but no-one who did the show seemed to go on to greater things. Perhaps it was because agents and bookers only saw you as being part of an enormous production and not as a solo performer. All that changed for me as I was leaving the stage door to rush off to my next gig one night. The stage doorkeeper gave me an envelope. Not thinking who it could be from, I opened it and read the message scribbled on it: *Dear Jon Jon, I really enjoyed your performance in the show and I wondered if you would like to join me on my TV show, singing and joining in with some of the sketches? Kind regards, Benny Hill.* I thought it was a gag - things like this did not happen to me. I shrugged it off, put the envelope in my pocket and rushed off to what was my reality: three more shows. Next day I opened the message and wondered, if it *was* real what did Benny want from me? At that day and age, any man of fifty who was not married was considered to be gay or at least suspect and, although Benny was always surrounded by beautiful girls, there was great conjecture about his sexual status. I hummed and harred for a couple of days and asked my wife what she thought I should do. She was of the opinion that anything I had to do to get her and three children out of a cold, damp caravan would be totally acceptable to her even if it meant that I might end up with a sore bum. I crossed my fingers said a prayer and telephoned Benny. 'Hello, dear heart,' a cheery voice said. 'I do hope

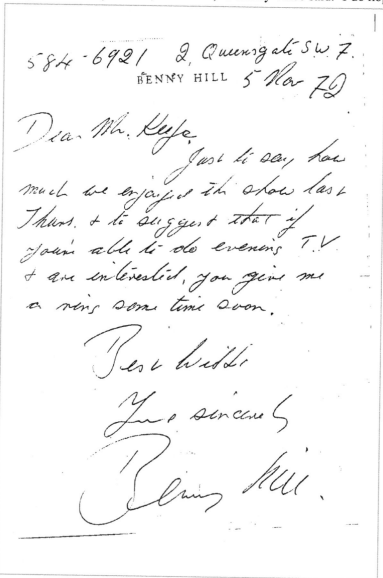

584-6921   2, Queensgate S.W. 7.
BENNY HILL   5 Nov 79

Dear Mr. Keefe,
            Just to say how
much we enjoyed the show last
Thurs. + to suggest that if
you're able to do evening T.V.
+ are interested, you give me
a ring some time soon.

            Best wishes
            Yours sincerely
            Benny Hill.

you are going to join us on the show. I would like you to bring along
one of the beautiful lady singers and do a duet on the show and learn
122

some of the sketches.'

It was as easy as that. Benny was a fully-fledged, roly-poly, beautiful 100% chap, kind, happy and just nice. As far as his sexuality was concerned, he was a mummy's boy, he loved his family. When asked why he never married he always said that if you owned and worked in a sweet shop you wouldn't only eat lemon drops, no you would have a suck and a chew on all the sweets in the store and so it was that he was surrounded by the most lovely girls in the business and never concentrated on just one of them.

My luck seemed to have changed. I thanked God for his timely intervention. It felt as though all my hardships and bad luck up until this point had been a trial of endurance and I seemed to have passed the test. So began nearly twenty years of the happiest time you could have standing up with your clothes on. I was still able to do the clubs at night and do the TV show in the day. The show was made at Thames TV at Teddington and all the running around in fields happened in the home counties, so I was able to do both gigs and help pay for builders to finish off the house.

17. Joining the Benny Hill Family

My first nerve-racking day was a 7 a.m. call in Green Park in Slough on a freezing cold November morning. It was so terrifying turning up on a film set of about a hundred cast and crew and not knowing anybody except the star who was deeply involved with producing the show. I felt put at ease by a cheery 'Morning J.J.' in the make-up caravan as Benny sat in the next chair. 'Hi Ben,' I said, rather shyly. He knew who I was and as he left he told the make-up girls to make me feel at home as I would be another member of the resident cast. I was made up and went on to the wardrobe caravan to be dressed as a German soldier in the First World War. I was fussed over and fondled by two major queens who were dressers, 'Welcome to the club. Ben's come up with a bit of eye candy instead of the gnarled characters we usually get to dress.' Over the years it seems I have been attractive to many gays in the business and I always say that they are without doubt the funniest most caustic raconteurs and I have never been taken advantage of or molested by any of them, except one, a speciality dancer, six foot two, muscles on muscles. Each night standing in the wings of The Talk of the Town, waiting to rush on to sing 'Ma Cherie Amore', with split-second timing this guy would crush my buns just as I was running on. Every night I swore I would get him back for it. One night his timing was off and I had time to crash a full-blooded punch into his chest. I ran on stage with a smile that soon faded as I heard him say with a lisp,

124

'OOOOH! Is that your best?' Fortunately it never happened again.

So, back to Slough. I walked on set dressed as this German soldier, alone and wondering what to do. But it wasn't long before I was greeted by a man in a German general's costume complete with spiked German helmet. A voice boomed out of the costume, 'Welcome to the show, dear boy,' and before I had time to be shocked I realised it was none other the famous Bob Todd, a huge comedy star, welcoming me to the show. I showed due deference to him which he brushed aside, 'I know how lonely film sets can be if you become a member of an already established cast and crew,' he said. He made me well at home, genned me up on where to go and what to do and then said, 'I wonder if you could see your way clear to lending me a

Jon Jon with Bob Todd

tenner as all my money is in my caravan and I need my dresser to get me a small libation, a half a bottle of whisky to fend off this aching cold from an old thespian's bones.' I hurriedly crushed the money into his hand and would have given him much more after making me feel so at home. He walked away to his dresser as two sparks walked past me saying, 'Hope you can afford to lose that. It's the last you'll see of it again.' I laughed and walked toward the set. No amount of money I spent on or leant to Toddy over the next nineteen years could have paid for the fun and laughter he gave me and the joy we had together.

The popularity of the show, the expense of putting it on and the brick bats from Mary Whitehouse and feminists and the problems Ben was having with different directors made the production very edgy. It was not like Ben to be difficult but some days he would not come out of his caravan until he got his way. This went on for several seasons with many changes of director until a dynamic little red-haired Geordie called Dennis Kirkland took over as director of the show.

Toddy Pays Out! :Dennis Kirkland [l], Benny [3ʳᵈ left], Bob Todd [5ᵗʰ left], Jon Jon [6ᵗʰ left] & Henry McGee [rt]

What a breath of fresh air. Ben and Den became like a double act. They agreed on most things and Den had a way of getting Ben to adjust and reconfigure his production expenses without affecting the result. Dennis had a pedigree of working with the best comedians in the business. He had produced the acclaimed *Plank*, a film about a building site with a whole host of comics trying their hardest to outdo each other's splendid performances and the removal men. He had worked with comics such as Tommy Cooper, Eric Sykes, Cannon and Ball and many, many more. Den knew what made comics tick and was equally as accomplished as a comedian himself. I grew to love this guy and he returned the favour by keeping me on the show. In showbusiness the cast members can become as part of your family, but one of the discomforting aspects of the biz is that the show invariably comes to an end and it feels like a very bad divorce – you may never work with those people again. That's why The Benny Hill Show was so special – we were together for sixteen years and the love and friendship just grew and grew.

18. My Heroes

Bob Todd, or Toddy as we called him, had been a Fresian cattle farmer of some renown and had gone into business with a bloke he thought was a gentleman farmer who had bought the next farm to his. He turned up with a big Range Rover, a speed boat and lots of flashy pieces of farm equipment. So when he approached Toddy to annex their herds, Toddy looked at all his accoutrements and thought it was a good idea. In fact, the man was a charlatan and Toddy found himself bankrupt. He found himself in his cups in his local and wondering what to do next.

Henry McGee, JonJon,Little Len & Bob Todd. [Photo: Thames Television]

The consensus of opinion amongst all that knew him was that with his great comical abilities he should go into showbusiness. This he did and he got a major role in a meat commercial saying 'It's Beef. It's Beef'. From this there followed a great career in comedy acting as stooge for some of the greatest comics as well as portraying some great character parts. Toddy loved a drink, that was self-evident. This was due, it appears, to some horrific experiences in the war. The extent of his drinking was only made evident in rehearsals as Ben wrote less and less dialogue for Toddy to learn and he ended up just being used in sketches where he just had to show his face and take his teeth out.

In rehearsals at the London Irish rugby club we were having a particularly difficult time learning a wordy sketch. We were working with Henry McGee, whom we revered as a proper thespian, myself, little Jackie Wright and Toddy. We had to be word perfect as Ben had written the words and there was no way of deviating from them without him knowing. Henry had the incredible ability to peruse a sheet of dialogue and, with photographic memory, memorize it in one slow read of the page. I marvelled at his incredible ability as I really had to struggle retaining dialogue. As a joke I would bow down in front of him and say, 'Hail, oh great purveyor of the written word!'

'Do rise up dear boy,' he would say with a flourish, 'for exaltations should be heaped on the cabaret performers, for if we actors are not furnished with the written word then there is a redundacy in our ability to act at all whilst you cabaret artistes are able to ad lib at will. Hail to thee.' And so it was that we shared a mutual admiration for each other for nineteen years.

Toddy was making hard-going of the rehearsals and could not get his dialogue right. We told him he was a drunken old has-been and he replied that, if it were not for the likes of him and other members of His Majesty's Royal Air Force… perhaps we should not be so dismissive of one of England's great flying heros. We agreed that

Douglas Bader deserved our utmost respect but we didn't see what that had to do with him. Later we found out what he had been talking about. One night he was coerced into going into the studio to take part in a *This is Your Life* for Barry Cryer presented by Eammon Andrews. It had been really tough keeping Toddy out of the bar but Den said he owed Barry a drink-free celebration of Barry's contribution to comedy. So Toddy sat next to Barry waiting for him to divulge a little anecdote or two. The look on Toddy's face when Eammon introduced him as 'Bob Todd, comedian, farmer, raconteur and R.A.F. Bomber' was priceless. We were all gob-smacked. In fact, Toddy had been decorated for his war efforts. He'd been shot down five times and had fought his way back through enemy lines to get back into the war. Our already incredible respect for such a nice man now soared. His dialogue, on the other hand, got less and less.

Rehearsals for the show were held around Teddington or Richmond, often at London Irish Rugby Club. They were demanding but great fun. The Hill's Angels would be put through really difficult routines and the girls would be used in sketches as well. The show was often slated by critics for being lewd and demeaning to women but nothing could be further from the truth. Ben loved and respected all of his young ladies and would help them to get on in the business. The irony was that most of them were heavily involved with their boyfriends who were invariably car salesmen or plumbers or such like. The rehearsal day would have the actors in one side of the rehearsal rooms learning the sketches and the girls attired in tight-fitting lycra perspiring profusely and we would have the groundsmen of the rugby club ogling them through the windows on the other side of the rehearsal rooms. Other men seemed amazed that we appeared to take no notice of these nubile, beautiful creatures and perhaps this gave substance to the myth that most men in showbusiness were gay. Maybe it's just that familiarity breeds contempt. One day, while we were rehearsing, a huge coach of erstwhile St Trinian's girls poured from a coach, dressed only in gym slips and carrying hockey sticks to play. The groundsmen pressed their noses against the window to see our lyca-clad belles and the whole male cast pressed their noses against the glass from the inside to admire the young girls running across the field. It was a Benny Hill sketch in itself!

19. Residuals

The sketches were all rehearsed in preparation for them to be shot in the studio. All the outside running-around bits were shot on location from November to February usually at Thorpe Park, a theme park that closed for the winter and had all the facilities we needed for sketches on roundabouts and rides and the like. I often found myself in a pair of Speedos in the depths of winter under big lamps to make it look as sunny as possible while being encouraged by my director, Mr Dennis Kirkland, to plunge in a freezing lake as part of a sunny beach scene. There was an on-going ruse of seeing who could pull the best gags on each other which went on for the whole life of the show. It was mandated that you had to come to work each day with a plan to pull an original gag, particularly on Den or a member of his back-up team. The gags never interfered with our work but were very important to keep us on our toes. Ben would not be a part of these goings-on, as he was totally absorbed in bringing the very best work to the screen. So, when I was asked to dive into a freezing lake, I always had to ask myself whether it was a ruse or not. There was a cry that went up that would have people scrambling to take your place to do it, even fighting off the advances of none other than the celebrated straight man himself, discarding clothes as he ran towards the director, Mr Henry McGee making himself available if I refused and that cry was 'Residuals'.

The show was being sold to a hundred countries around the world, its slapstick, clean-cut English postcard burlesque was loved and celebrated from France to Switzerland and as far away as America. But in England it was dismissed by Mary Whitehouse and The Womens' Institute for being lewd and sexist. Ben was admonished for portraying a dirty old man chasing scantily-clad young ladies around a field. The people who criticised the show obviously didn't watch it because otherwise they would know that the girls chased Benny and us and invariably wacked a custard pie in our face for even pretending to be dirty old men. The irony once again was that if these critics had asked the young

Jon Jon, Jenny Lee Wright, Benny Hill & Jackie Wright [Photo courtesy of Thames TV]

ladies in question they would have been told in no uncertain words to mind their own business, it was good clean fun. The language and the filth that passes for humour now is a whole different subject matter for a book in itself.

Anyway, back to residuals. Each time you appeared in a programme that was shown on TV in the United Kingdom or anywhere else in the world, you would pick up a percentage of your

133

original fee, this was called a residual, and because of this word Mr Dennis Kirkland could encourage his performers to attempt things that were outside the scope of their acting or physical ability. So, without having to call in stunt men or other specialised performers, by the mere loud exclamation of the word 'residuals', he had available to him a baying eager crowd of nutters.

It was now 1974, I was still busy working on the house, coming to the end of the contract at The Talk of the Town and working on The Benny Hill Show. Life was a blur. I just went from one gig to another with bags of energy to accomplish all that lay before me. Although I had worked at The Talk of the Town for over a year, it was still necessary for me to audition for a role in the new show. I know I had been well regarded in the production I was currently in but was still required to audition again. I did this without the fear and trepidation that I felt the first time I auditioned though mounting the stage of the Talk and peering out into the black auditorium, hearing nothing but disjointed voices from behind a distant light, was still a little nerve-wracking. 'OK J.J., what have you got for us?' a camp Canadian voice called from behind the light. Billy Petch with his assistant Bobbie and Mr Robert Nesbitt and his assistant Miss Ros Wilder were just discernable in the half-light. I had heard that the new show was going to have a circus theme so I told them I was going to do a ballad and an audience participation song. The ballad was 'Somewhere' from *West Side Story* and the join in number was 'Mame'. The ballad was well-received and I started 'Mame' wearing a straw boater. Over the intro I requested that each time I removed my hat all assembled had to shout 'Mame'. So I started: "You coaxed the blues right out of the horn, Mame..." Nothing. I stopped the pianist and said to the assembled panel of judges that it was really important for them to show a little willing to extract the best from my performance. We started again and I laughed inside as I heard the cut-glass tones of Mr Nesbitt and the rest of his cohorts singing "Mame". After I had finished my audition and was leaving the stage, Big John, the Talk's sound engineer, whispered as he walked past me to reset the microphone, 'That's a first J.J. No-one has ever got any of the Nuremberg trial judges to join in.'

20. A Terrible Blow!

I needed the show at The Talk to run with The Benny Hill Show. Neither of them paid very well, so it was necessary to do the two of them together to make up a decent wage. I waited for a reply from The Talk and was told I had been pencilled in. This was a great relief as I also waited from news about a new Benny Hill contract. A month turned into six weeks and everything was winding down, so I phoned The Talk to ask when the rehearsal dates were. I was told by Miss Ros Wilder that the management had changed their minds and that I was not now being considered for the next production. In showbiz as much as you would love to scream at these people who hold your destiny in their hand, you cannot do so as the certain fact is that you would not work for them again. So I had to accept the news whilst biting my bottom lip and saying jauntily, 'OK, next time then.' This was a terrible blow, especially as I had not heard from The Benny Hill Show. I paced around the telephone wondering if I should call Benny. My better judgement said not to. With big organisations like TV companies, I knew that decisions were driven so much by politics that even the stars were not in control of their own destinies. My dear wife, who had had some experience in the modelling world, watched me fret and worry. She said that we needed to know, so I should just phone and find out what was happening so that we could make arrangements with our own lives. I prevaricated and, against my better judgement, phoned Benny. As soon as he answered the phone with his usual 'Hello J.J., dear heart,' I knew that I had made the wrong decision. I told him I was just phoning to find out if I were to be included in the next series. But, unbeknown to me, Ben was fighting for his own life on the show due to the big production costs that show incurred. I heard his genial voice change to one of concern, 'Er, er… I know not, dear boy. These things are arranged by the casting department.' As his flustered voice trailed off I apologised profusely for having bothered him and put down the phone. I was not included in the next series and life was going to get tough once again.

It was November 1974, I was working like mad on the house and naively decided to knock the windows out. When I went to get them replaced the guy told me it would take three months. So here we were with no work coming in, no windows in the house and five of us still living the caravan. There was nothing to it, I had to get a job. A friend of mine owned an exhibition company, making all the stands at motercycle and motor car shows. I asked him if I could work for him and, like many people I knew, he was surprised that I needed a job, when they knew I was on TV and working in nightclubs. You never demeaned yourself by telling people how little money acts of my position earned in the biz and we brushed it off by pretending that we all lived up to the hilt. Of course, in most cases this was not true. So I started working in the day time humping sheets of eight foot by four foot chipboard about, up and down narrow openings in the Grosvenor House Hotel, Earls Court, Wembley Conference Centre. It was tough. I was tested by the guys I worked with as I had to prove that this erstwhile star could still do a decent day's work. One day we moved nine hundred sheets of chipboard through a really narrow doorway. Frank and John were two great Irish labourers, tough and funny, and we started to move the boards at first one by one, they said if we quickened it up we could go to the cafe for breakfast. They started to pick up two boards at a time, so of course I followed suit. Two eight by four sheets of chipboard are really heavy and working them through a small doorway was backbreaking. We finished the task and they roared with laughter as we went off for a hard-earned breakfast. I asked what the joke was and they roared as they said they never ever moved two boards at a time. I had passed the test.

21. My 'Gangster' Show

So I was working really hard in the daytime and I was still trying for club dates in the evening. *The Astor, Churchills, The Boulogne* in Chinatown, *The Celebrity, The Latin Quarter, The Stork Room* dens of entertainment. I would find myself running from one gig to another across Regent Street in the wee small hours of the morning from one club to another as another singer would be running in the opposite direction.

'How is your crowd?' I'd yell.

'Crap.' invariably came the answer.

I had never worked *The Astor* in Berkeley Square before although I had been a customer when I was about eighteen with my car dealer friends Terry Clements, Johnnie Braine, Ernie Felgate and Eddie Pillar. The club was almost neutral territory for the Krays, the Richardsons, the Frasers and the Nashes. I had worked in pubs and clubs in all the different gangs' manors, of course in the East End and south of the river at The Thomas à Beckett run by Joe Lucey and the Savoy at Catford so I knew the sort of place it was.

The atmosphere at The Astor when one or more of the gangs were in was electric. They docked their guns in the cloakroom and tried not to eyeball members of the opposing gangs. The tension could be cut with a knife and you had to be experienced in knowing how not to upset the different factions. My friend was the drummer at the club and got me the gig. He gave me a sound piece of advice: 'Sing *"Bye*

Bye, Blackbird" but break off the first verse and say the only person who could do the song justice was Big Jimmy.' Now that song was a nightclub anthem and Jimmy was a six foot six henchman for the Krays. Once I'd broken off the song, I would invite Jimmy to come on stage and show me and all in the room how the song should be sung. This wise move not only ingratiated me with the management but got me in with Jimmy who gave orders that I was to be booked back at the club when ever there was a date available.

Despite what it sounds like, London was really quite a safe place. Soho, where most of the clubs were situated, was as safe a place to walk about in the wee small hours of the morning as anywhere. So everyone went about their work with a hurry in their step and no worry for one's safety. The sex trade was just beginning to bloom and even the prostitutes and their minders were friendly and happy-go-lucky if they knew you were in their biz of getting money off the wide-eyed punters. It paid to play up to the girls' more tender sides by singing them their favourite songs, usually sad and forlorn numbers. Move them and they got the punters to appreciate your show.

Soho was awash with characters. One such character was the doorman at Jack Isow's club in Berwick Street. It was a difficult job especially on nights when hundreds of northern rugby fans came down to London for the Rugby Cup Final. There would be a sea of drunken fans milling around Soho. The doorman's name was Nosher Powell and he was an ex-cruiserweight champion of Great Britain. He was a mountain of a man and a formidable doorman and a filmstunt man to boot. The story goes that Mr Jack Isow's son was concerned that there had been too much violence for even Nosher to handle on his own so, for the sake of Nosher and the club, he was going to get a dog handler to assist Nosher in his duties. Nosher was not best pleased as he said his relationship with dogs was not very good and that the dogs could smell the dislike Nosher had for them. Mr Jack said it was not to be a permanent arrangement, just on the hour every hour, the dog handler and his Alsation would walk around the block to other clubs, wait a while then move on. Nosher was still unconvinced of the need, but agreed to try it out. As soon as the dog turned up, Nosher shot down into the kitchen to get it some cuts of choice beef, which he would gingerly feed to the dog to let him know whose side he was on. This seemed to be working well until the first big fracas. A group of Scottish rugby fans decided they wanted to come into the club and, as diplomatically as possible, Nosher tried to dissuade them. All his talking was to no avail as two of them rushed the door. Quick as a flash Nosher knocked one of them out and battered the other down the stairs. He was still confronted by four other guys with even more intent on getting at Nosher. The dog handler turned up and Nosher used the chance to appeal to the four guys not make a move or that one word from him and the dog would be on them. They stepped forward and Nosher gave a signal to let the dog go. It snarled and jumped on Nosher and ripped his jacket to shreds. The Scotsmen could not believe their eyes and collapsed with laughter. The incident forgotten, Nosher changed his jacket and the dog never returned.

'Songs to Eat your Soup by'

I was now a permanent member of the songs to eat your soup by brigade but something came along that drove me harder to move on. I had managed to get an audition with Joe Loss' Big Band at The London Coliseum. The night before, my brother had pestered me to go out with him on his birthday. I should have listened to that little voice inside that said no, instead I said yes. We started off in the East End and ended up in a club in Chelsea. We were all the worse for wear and my brother even more so. I took the responsibility of letting one of the other guys drive home, he was a little less the worse for wear. But, coming back over Canning Town Bridge at 3 a.m., he clipped the corner of some roadworks and the car turned over. Fate being what it is, there were six of us in the car and, as it rolled, five flew out of the doors. Fortunately the last guy out was holding onto me and pulled me in as my head went through a side window. The car rolled several times and I was the only one in it. It came to a halt and I was taken out by the ambulance men and taken to Poplar hospital where I remained with a fractured neck and twenty-four stitches in my head. I was in a plastercast for months and eventually was fitted with a neck brace. The importance to me was only to become evident later. Prior to this I had been a stickler for the way I looked, mohair-suited, sleeked-back Cary Grant-type hair, the biz. I was very shy and very fussy about the way I looked. Until one day, standing at a bus stop, a

142

little girl said to her mother, 'Mum, what's that man got that funny hat on for?' I stopped being shy that day realising that I had been taking myself too seriously. Fate played its hand again.

One night I went back to The Fiddlers again. I had been in Sweden and learned the secret of how to get girls. All you had to do was talk to them. This was something you didn't learn growing up in the East End. Most guys were shy and fell into relationships with girls by a fluke. You could see a girl you liked and it took ages to buck up the courage to pull her. So week after week you would just show out and eventually ask her if she wanted a drink or a dance and a meal. Going away taught me to take the bull by the horns and just ask straight away. These were stunning looking creatures and I was having some success. Unfortunately I did this when I came home and had forgotten the code that I would have been stuck with, had I not gone away. Seeing a girl I liked the look of, I broke off from the guys and asked if she would like a drink. I arrived back with a gin and tonic and all hell let loose. Some hard nutter had considered her to be his girl even though he had never spoken to her. Moving away from the East End made me forget some of the codes of practice. I went into the pub one evening to see some guy called Soapy Clarke slapping my brother about and all the guys taking very little notice of what was going on. I was not a fighter nor a coward so I ran to give my brother some assistance but, as I went to throw a punch at the guy, it was my brother who stopped me, explaining it was nothing to do with me. One thing led to another and more people joined in as the brawl burst out onto the pavement. My kid brother was in the centre of the brawl and I was looking for a suitably skinny guy to punch. As I ran at the guy I'd chosen, I came to a swift and sudden halt as he pulled a gun out of his pocket and thrust it under my chin. I was suspended in the air as I heard him pull back the pin, only to be saved by my brother saying to the guy that I spent too much time around film stars. The outcome of the brawl was that this gang of guys were winding themselves up adrenaline-wise and went off to rob the local cinema of its takings.

Banged-up in Southend Nick

Each time I went back home to my roots I seemed to get caught up in some ongoing bit of local politics that I knew nothing about. So an innocent night out at The Basildon Palais dancing to The Dave Clark Five, before they were really famous, resulted in a huge fight and a return match with a local gang of guys smashing up The Palais and retreating to a hotel in Raleigh. I didn't have a clue what was going on and stayed out of the melée. It was only when we were on the way home, as the guys shared stories of their escapades, that we were stopped by the Southend Police, a force to themselves, and taken to Southend nick where I spent the night in a cell. I know where I was when President Kennedy died – banged up in Southend nick. We were charged and I went away again swearing to myself that I had to sever the ties with my roots or else I could end up in the nick for longer next time. It took a long time to bring the case to court as I was always abroad. When I did get back to go to court with the other six guys, the judge threatened us with riotously assembling and causing an affray, an offence against the crown, punishable by seven to fifteen years in prison. As it was, for circumstances known only to the court, I got off with a £15 fine. Needless to say I did not go home again. God Bless British Justice.

The people I grew up with were not exactly villains, they just seemed to get into trouble from what started off as a laugh. I entertained villains and I knew the difference. The atmosphere could change at the drop of a hat, with some misunderstanding of a look or a gesture or a supposed slight. The West End was controlled by different sets of villains and you had to know who they were. If they liked you they were generous to a fault and you felt protected. The nightclubs were a place where they went to have a good time and it was important for an entertainer to know the whys and wherefors of different people. Dedicate a song, make a fuss of wives and mothers, make no sign of the fact that they may have been in the club even the night before with a girlfriend. Total integrity, that only a London street-cred education could give you. I have seen other performers who were not aware of the importance of being able to be affable and intelligent of the politics of club life, come unstuck by a glib remark or a cheap aside, not knowing the reputation of who he might be getting a cheap laugh from. Most villains have a fragile sense of humour but a wicked sense of embarrasment. Do not go near either of these highly toxic subjects.

Villains like to put on a good show, make a big splash of being up the front of a nightclub revelling in their notoriety. A gentle acknowledgement of their notoriety is OK. Invariably they would like to sit ringside with family and friends and back up in the dark with lovers and cohorts. With this in mind and without him knowing it, a well-known star came to The Starlight and part of his act was ridiculing people sitting near the front of the stage. This guy is now seriously in trouble and finds it hard to get work. Without him knowing it, I almost saved his life when one night he did what he always did which was insist that a person he did not like the look of should get up and leave the table he was sitting at. I saw this happening and knew the night was going to get very tricky from then on. Without knowing it, the guy he had chosen to ridicule and send out was a serious villain. He chided him in front of his large party on the front table, manhandling him and physically escorting him away from the stage to the bar area. This whole act was accompianied by roars of laughter from the crowd, but viewed very seriously by myself, the band, the management and the other customers who knew who the star had picked on. The star escorted the immaculately-dressed customer to the bar, which was about a hundred feet away, to roars of laughter. I made my way to the place where he deposited him and, as the star went back to the stage, persuaded the furiously embarrassed man to join me at the bar for a bottle of champagne as a token of our respect and as a rejection of such a cheap trick. The man spoke of having the star severly injured because of his embarrassment. I was

146

most concerned that it did not happen on the premises and that he should make any arrangements he wished to deal with this pillock away from The Starlight. Our star was not a nice person so, while at least he didn't get hurt that night, later his career crashed sensationally.

Who would have thought that a young boy with very little going for him could find himself in such exalted company, sitting in the pictures listening to Mario Lanza sing, 'Because you're mine, the brightest star I see is shining down on me, because you're mine'.

Of all the big stars – Frank Sinatra, Sammy Davis Jnr., Tony Bennett, Mel Torme, Johnny Mathis, Billy Daniells, Billy Eckstine - I worked with everyone except Frank Sinatra. I did a season with a comic called Joe Church whose trick was to come on stage with a plank of wood and tell jokes about it and use it as a prop. It was a thrill swapping stories of when he compèred a show at The London Palladium with Frank Sinatra. I was eager to know what Frank was like. Joe said he didn't know even though he spent a week on the bill with him. He would say, 'Ladies and Gentlemen, Mr Frank Sinatra,' and the stage door would open and Frank would step out of his limo walk on stage do his act and leave the same way. Joe never met him.

Variety was the spice of life. Acts met up and hacked about their experiences. There were plenty of harrowing stories of being robbed by crooked agents and berated by uncaring and drunken audiences, the outcome was always a hilarious story of some awful situation. These stories of trial and tribulation became the cement that glued you to each other; only the few who were artists knew what was going on. Dashing up and down motorways, getting paid off, dying in front of audiences: this was the grist of life as a variety artiste.

A favourite haunt in the early days was Lyon's Corner House on Newport Street in London. Acts old and new went there for cheap meals and endless cups of tea and to pick up gigs from other acts. If that failed, we would go to the pictures where it was warm and more comfortable than the damp digs we lived in and in those days you could stay all day.

22. Comedy is not all laughs

There were enormous hazards in being a singer but the toughest, loneliest trade was that of a comedian. Comedians could be a huge success on one show and die the next even though it was the same material, same delivery, same act. Dying on stage is the loneliest experience there is. At least with the music playing you don't walk off to the sound of your own footsteps. Comedy seems to have gone through an enormous transformation over the years. It seems that things that were once thought to be funny may not be now. Broad, slapstick humour, or subtle play on words and nuances are no longer the order of the day. In those days, comedians were segregated into two types of comics: those who said funny things and those who said things funny. The first group could learn the lines, but the second group had an innate sense of comedy that was beyond explanation – these were men like Tommy Cooper, Max Wall, Ken Dodd and Norman Collier. Without saying a word these guys could make you laugh.

A comic could travel around the country doing his act and it might be a couple of years before he came back to the same theatre, which meant that when he did come back the audience was treated to an act that had a few more gags added to it, and what was already there was more finely honed, so he knew exactly where and how the laughs would come. Prior to his show his act would be vetted by someone from the local council to make sure it had no swearing in it or any references to body parts or such. So that on the night of the performance what he presented to his audience was full of innuendo or double entendre and the programme would have them splitting their sides with laughter without the comedian swearing or being filthy. This was what separated the comics from those who had to resort to filth and banality to be the artists they became. In my view the need for filth and swearing on all of the media now has it seems made it possible for anyone to consider themselves as comics. The difference between some unfunny guy in a smart suit delivering learned lines, and a bawdy comic like Alan Carr who looks like he has lived and experienced life as Alan Carr is where the comedy lies.

A comic of great reknown in the biz was Norman Collier. Norman was an authentic, one-off funny man. Comics with less talent would avoid him as his conversation reminded them what a true comic he was and what an innate talent that was. Norman had several of his funny remarks and mannerisms stolen by other well-known

Jon Jon with Norman Collier

comedians. His famous broken 'ackerred microphone' gag was just one of the jokes other comedians copied. Without knowing it, it seemed Norman has the ability to talk about himself in the third person, strangely explaining things that happen to him as if it were someone else. He once told me a story about having finished a sucessful night at a club in Leeds.

He was driving himself home in the wee small hours of the morning in a recently purchased Jaguar. 'Well, another great night of humour under your belt Norman. Thee haven't done bad driving across t' moors on t' way home to t'lovely house. Proud, in fact thee should be. Proud.'

Rounding a bend in a narrow lane in the Derbyshire moors he spooked a deer or something, slammed on the brakes and ended up upside down on a dry-stone wall. 'Oh Norman, what have thee done lad? Pride coming before a fall. Don't panic. Where are thee? Right, it appears you're upside down, hanging from the seatbelt and you can smell petrol and there's something dripping. Could it be blood Norman? Now don't panic, get out of the seatbelt and get theeself out of t'car. Easier said than done, Norman. I think t'leg is broken as it's pointing in a funny way. Breath in deeply and ease theeself up from t' belt and click it hard. Oooh, oooh. thee've done it but thee've crashed t' roof. Thee have now to pull theeself out of t' window. The pain, Norman. Don't panic, don't panic. Argh!' With that Norman heard the sound of voices coming towards the car out of the darkness.

'Eh oop, old lad, what have thee gone and managed to have done? Why it looks like a brand new car.'

'Aye, it is,' says Norman. 'Is this your wall?'

'Aye lad, it is.'

'Sorry about t' wall,' says Norman.

'Never thee mind lad. Let's get thee away from here before it goes up in flames.'

Having extracted Norman through the window they realised he had a broken leg. 'Eee lad. this does not look good. We've to get thee back to t' farm across t' field to phone an ambulance. We've to make a stretcher. Use a couple of my jackets. Put t' branches through t' sleeves and put me on 'em.'

This they did and it wasn't until they got within the light of the farmhouse that one of them recognised Norman. 'Here, our Billy, have thee seen who we have on t' stretcher?'

'No Harry. Who?'

'It's 'im off t' telly. The carpark man. "Hello, microphone's ackerred." It's 'im.'

They got him inside the house and put him down on the floor, his leg bloodied and broken and, before calling the ambulance, they called upstairs, 'Mother! Eh, mother, you'll never guess who we have down 'ere. It's Norman Collier off t' telly.'

Norman was asked to open the cabaret at a brand-new refurbished quarter-of-a-million pound miners' socialclub in Yorkshire. Being one of their own, the committee wanted only Norman for the opening night. Although they had spent a fortune on the club and bar, Norman said he walked onto a huge stage and stood unable to move left or right, under a pathetic watery light and had to deliver his act into what amounted to a Woolworth's tannoy system. Norman said the act was a struggle and when the social secretary came to give him his money, he expressed his own and the committee's opinion of a very, very poor performance. Club secretaries and committees were a law unto themselves, and for them ignorance was bliss. There were an awful lot of blissfully happy club secrataries with a fortune to spend on entertainment and not a clue as to what it took to be successful.

Another comedian who frightened lesser talents was Frank Carson. Frank didn't put on an act – he was a walking non-stop verbal portrayer of mirth. If you heard 'It's the way I tell 'em' in the bar, Frank would be off on a non-stop verbal marathon and no-one could get a word in. His booming Northern Irish brogue would ring out, 'Jon Jon, the world's gone PC mad. I did a gig at the Walthamstow Town Hall the other night and there were students outside with banners saying "No Irish Jokes". I leaned out of the dressing room window and said, 'D'you not know that I'm Irish? You're taking the food out of my children's mouths.'

A typical Frank joke was: 'In Belfast today an RUC police Panda car collided with a tree and three officers were seriously injured. The I.R.A. said they planted the tree. It's the way I tell 'em. Frank Carson, News at Ten, Walthamstow.'

23. The Starlight Room

Compere to The Stars

I had finished all my resident nightclub work in London and now had time to select other, better paying, dates due to my appearances on The Benny Hill Show. I went for an audition at a brand-new five-hundred seater cabaret restaurant in Enfield called, not very originally, The Starlight Club. I could not know that this short booking of a month would keep me employed for the next twenty-five years, on and off. I was originally hired as the host and compère and eventually became the cabaret director, responsible for hiring all of the biggest names in the entertainment business. The owner of the club was a charlatan. I had met many characters in my time but this man proved to be a total one-off. He was a short, rotund, elegant erstwhile builder. His main preoccupation away from building was to become the director of one of the most famous amateur football teams

154

in England: Enfield Town F.C. They were a successful club but he assured them they needed cash from a source other than football as the gates of even a successful club like Enfield could not support the plans he had to make the club even bigger. So, without planning permission, he erected a five-hundred seat nightclub restaurant next to the football pitch. He was a charming man when he needed to be, but an out and out villain when he needed to be too. He fought the existing football club committee on his plans and proposals and none of them had the courage to fight his plans for putting up such a large building without planning permission. Nobody knew how he was able to accomplish this and when it was finally challenged, he persuaded the council that no other borough had such an impressive establishment. It was, in fact, a jewel in their crown. He was determined to make it one of the best nightclub restaurants in the country.

Eartha Kitt gets the 'push'

His persuasive tactics obviously worked as the mayor and the town council were invited to a gala charity night with a six course meal and a cabaret by Eartha Kitt. Miss Kitt has a formidable presence and she let myself and the band know who she was and how she wished to be presented. She was a formidable diva and we trod carefully around her. During my long career, I have had the experience of escorting not one but two formidable stars: one onto the stage and one off the stage, both as a result of gargling too much mouthwash (otherwise known as booze) prior to their performance. Miss Kitt gargled with only the

155

finest brandy which, it seems, made it all the more potent. She came to the end of her famous song 'Old-Fashioned Millionaire' laying on a chaise-longue and appearing to be nodding off. I was summoned by the owner to do something. I did not know who to be more fearful of, an irate evening-suited builder or a temperamental she-cat. He pushed me through the curtains on the side of the stage and I emerged infront of a puzzled crowd. I signalled for the band to play some 'get off' music and proceeded to push the chaise-longue with Miss Kitt on it off stage right, trying to make it look as much a part of the act as possible, all without waking her up. I seemed to have done this successfully and, just as we rounded the curtains, she awoke and shouted at me as loud as she could. I scarpered, leaving her to be dealt with by her own minders.

The lady I had to push *onto* stage was also a formidable diva: Miss Dorothy Squires. Miss Squires arrived early at the club for a band call. It was 4 p.m. and she was with her niece. The run-through with the band was fine and she and her niece were made comfortable in the dressing room. After a time they became bored and, with time to kill as the show didn't start until 10.30 p.m., they decided to leave to visit the Mayor of Enfield. They were missing for a long time and show time was getting near. Then the stage door was flung open and Miss Squires and her niece came in, three sheets to the wind. She had been gargling large amounts of champagne. I found them spread out on the dressing room floor roaring with laughter. I tried to tell them that it was almost time to go on, but all my prompting fell on deaf ears. I didn't know what to do other than summon up copious amounts of black coffee and implore them to get ready. Show time was late and the owner was going mad at me for keeping the customers waiting. I told him of the condition of Miss Squires and kept the band playing until I could see that she was almost ready and I could go on for my compère slot. So there I was with a formidable Welsh diva highly intoxicated backstage and I was coming to the end of my spot. Top of my mind was how to get her on stage without letting the audience know how pissed she was. I finished my final song to a decent round of applause and announced the star of the show. A drum roll started and the band struck up Miss Squires' opening song. I walked back into the wings and, as faultlessly as possible, deposited Miss Squires at the centre-stage mike. I need not have bothered with covering up her condition as the first words she said before I was even off stage were 'How are you, you English bastards?' A roar went around the crowd – they knew they were in for a most unusual evening's entertainment. She was a wild success.

Covering up for the Stars

I don't know how I became a compère, it just kind of crept up on me. Most of the time it was most ungratifying. I had to go on to an audience who had been kept waiting and often could not explain what the problem had been. I usually did a forty-minute spot in which time people would be walking around, ordering drinks and mainly waiting for the star of the show. No matter how good you were, you only had so long to impress an audience who didn't know who you were, especially if it was their first time in the club. So my act had an accompaniment of chatter and clinking glasses until the crowd had settled down and caught the last ten minutes of my act and realised how good I was. It was a tough spot but I was much appreciated by the top of the bill as I would always first vet their material to make sure I never ventured into their act. I learned that if a straight singer was on I should do some gags and maybe a few impressions, and if a comic was on, I would do a programme of songs. I even learned to juggle just in case. Some of the newer guys paid no deference to the top of the bill and sometimes even went on to see if they could take the shine off the star doing some of their jokes. Because of the time I had spent in the business, I had learned to be respectful of the act who came on last as it was they who created the draw to fill up the place. Plus I never stopped being star struck. I just loved the business I was in so much. As a compère I had to cover up for any number of acts that never turned up, acts that were late and acts that were just plain crap. I would never let on to the audience that there was trouble backstage. My job was to make it appear as though it was a well-oiled show and hide all the trials and tribulations going on backstage.

Some well-known names whom we paid thousands of pounds to appear were just not worthy of the fame and rewards that had been thrust upon them. Striving to get to the top of the bill had been their sole aim in life and, more times than not, they soon forgot how fortunate they had become. It's true to say that the acts that had come up the hard way through travelling the country year in year out were not so affected. They tended to remember how hard the slog had been and thanked their lucky stars that they were now successful. These people were a joy to be around but the acts that had become overnight sensations on television were the worst.

I had earned a great deal of respect from the regular members of the club. I was known for making such a great fuss on their mother's birthday, weddings, anniversaries, christenings, barmitzvahs. You name it, I was there. I was really busy at the club but not always happy. I had argued several times with the intransigent, ignorant owner and had even left a couple of times because he was becoming more and more difficult. He refused to re-invest some of the great money he was making into updating all the lighting and sound equipment. The club was running on a rubber band and I had enough to contend with just dealing with difficult acts and musicians. I went off to Jersey to do a summer season and to finish off building my house and, in my absence, the members of the club had a petition to get me back to the club. Several names had been employed to take my place but none of them proved successful.

Director, Agent & Performer

So when I received a call asking me to come back I wasn't too surprised. I knew what a difficult call it must have been to make so I went to lunch knowing I was in the strongest bargaining position I had ever been in in my career. I went armed with a list of things I wanted if I were to come back. Sound, lights and a greatly increased salary. The owner was tough to bargain with but threw in a position I had not expected: the agent of the club had died and the owner thought we should start our own in-house agency. He suggested that I should take up the post as I knew what the club needed better than anybody. This was a whole new thing for me for, although I had been in the business for such a long time, agents and agency business was a whole different ball game. I pondered on it and he said he would make me a director of the club with a car, increased salary, mobile phone, everything thrown in. I had always felt like a dogsbody in the business, with no control over my destiny at all. This was the first time I would have control over what I loved the best, being in showbiz. I accepted and took on a learning curve that was tiring though exciting. I had to learn fast. I was dealing with some of the biggest agents in the biz and they could eat you for supper if you didn't know what you were up to. I had to learn about contracts, fees, riders, get-out clauses. I had started out wanting to sing for a living and be paid for it, here I was now speaking to the agents I had been unable to get to return my calls when I was just an entertainer and they were now asking me to engage their artists.

It is difficult to imagine again being an East End lad, having failed his 11-plus, with a future that looked pretty grim, with little hope of my dreams coming true. Now here I was appearing on stage in front of an audience of rich and important people, not only appearing with the one and only Tony Bennett, but having booked the whole show

160

myself. The night was electric. I went on stage and settled the audience down. I was well-received and was congratulated by Mr Bennett's manager for setting the evening up so well. Mr Bennett came on and delivered a performance of over thirty songs and

received a raptuous reception. The evening was a huge success.

Booking acts for a nightclub was much more difficult than I expected. We were open fifty-two weeks a year, but it was financially impossible to engage top

Tony Bennett with Jon Jon

name acts every week for the money that their managements were asking. So, although it was showbiz, we were still subjected to the commercial market of supply and demand. Once your members have become used to seeing the very best acts they expect the very best. Even with the money we could charge for a very good three course meal, after the band's and the star's salary, sometimes we only had the takings from the bar to make a profit or sometimes just break even. It's difficult to believe but there were only about fifteen acts in the whole of the cabaret scene that could guarantee a full house. And we would be competing with other clubs with a much bigger clientele than we had. Some were a thousand seaters, so we had to charge more with fewer patrons. Because of the size of the club, the room was much more intimate and atmospheric and the patrons and the stars who appeared there both enjoyed that. So, on top of the great Tony Bennett, some of our greatest nights were cabarets by Jimmy Tarbuck and his sidekick Kenny Lynch. Jimmy loved the club and did a show that raised the roof. I could get him to come back to appear at the club whenever he was available, which for us was never often enough as he was so busy. Another great hit at the club was the much maligned performer, great comic and entertainer, Bob Monkhouse. He came across all creamy and insincere on TV and everybody in the business agreed without doubt that he was the master at presenting game shows and variety shows. In cabaret he was

Jon Jon with Jimmy Tarbuck

a totally different performer: funny, caustic and saucy. Showering the audience with ad-libs and brilliant repartee, he was brilliant.

As star-struck as I was, I still found I could feel let down by someone I really admired so when someone lived up to your expectations, it was magic. Bob was one such person. He had the knack of making everyone in the club feel appreciated. He had a list of all the people who worked at the club and genned up on it when next he came to work there. So it was that he got out of the car and said the name of whoever he came in contact with, even down to the carpark attendant, Lennie, who was a wizened little authoritarian who took no truck with anybody be they stars or customers. Upset Lennie

Jon Jon with Bob Monkhouse

and you could find yourself parked right down the carpark in a puddle. Bob always said, 'Hello Len' and Lennie and everybody else who Bob happened to know the name of, sang the praises of Mr Monkhouse as being a very nice man. Bob was so shrewd and left nothing to chance. He would greet me like a long-lost friend and smack a kiss on my cheek. I would tell him who was in the club so that if he needed to he could direct some material at them and make them feel even more special. He really did his homework.He was renowned for presenting company celebrations, getting there early and finding out who the characters in the firm were, what their position in the company was and directing his whole act as if it had been written for the product launch or in-house company celebration. But the strange thing with him was that all the applause and plaudits never seemed to be enough. He always seemed to be wanting more acceptance and adulation; it was difficult to put your finger on why. My nose was put out by him only once when he came to do a gig. We had worked together at the club many times and I know how he respected me. I greeted him the same as always, told him who was in, assured him that I had employed all his favourite musicians and told him what a great draw he was for the club. As I was leaving to start the show he said, 'J.J., dear heart, please do me a favour. Last time I was here I didn't feel that I went as well as usual, so could you please temper some of your comedy or maybe not do any gags at all and just sing?' I had a difficult enough job getting the audience to take any notice of me as it was let alone tying my hands behind my back and throwing me to the lions. I stopped, turned to look at his smiling face, paused and then tutted – a most unnerving sound of dismay to a performer. I walked out of the dressing room wondering just how much applause one man needed. He had money and fame and I had to fight for any kind of recognition at all. He walked on to total acclaim, he was highly paid, and he still wanted me to make it easier for him at my own expense. I did what he asked me though and he totally lost my respect. It happened a great deal with many so-called stars.

24. My Short Life as a Recording Artist

One day, out of the blue, I got a phone call from an independent record producer. He and his fellow producer had been to the club to look at another act and had liked what I did more. Disco was huge by this point and they wanted to use me on a disco record they had written. I was amazed that they could see the potential in me and got in touch with them immediately. They had a office in Wardour Street, London and I made arrangements to see them. They presented me with music I had not been used to singing but with a great deal of hard work they coached me in the art of recording. It was completely different from live performing, more

Hollywood Brown

breathy, more controlled. The song they had written was called 'Love on the American Express'. I signed a contract with them and they went to work producing the record. They persuaded me to change my name for recording purposes to 'Hollywood Brown'. The record got good notices from several recording companies and they ended up signing with Bronze Records. Bronze had some really big recording names on their books chiefly Manfred Mann and Osibisa.

165

We went to their offices in Camden Town and I was taken into a large boardroom, placed on a chair in the middle of the room and my managers and the recording executives sat around me deciding on my recording future. They came up with a new record producer who they had flown in from Australia and decided on a plan of action. I turned to my managers for advice and, as hard bitten as they were, having had a whole wall of their office plastered with tapes that had either bitten the dust, or were under discussion with record companies that amounted to thousands of pounds and they said this was the real deal. We were over the moon.

We went into the studio and cut the finished record. The company released it and I was driving to the club one day and heard it being played on Tony Blackburn's Radio One Hot Plays show. I had been waiting for years for something as good as this to happen. My managers were ecstatic as it meant they would be able to recoup some of the money they had spent on all the previous productions they had made. Plans were going ahead with club dates and interviews and building a career as Hollywood Brown. With airplays still ongoing, I received a call from my managers. It was one of those ominous calls. They asked me to meet with them in London. And, when I got there, it turned out that the owner of Bronze Records was upset at his wife flying around the world with their acts on their private jets and so he was going to cut back his involvement with the company. In fact, in no time at all he had sold the company to Chris Blackwell of Chrysalis Records. Chrysalis had a policy that did not include disco as they focussed more on the acts like Bob Marley that they represented. My managers pleaded that the record we had produced was getting lots of airplay and, with a push from the company, it would be a success. Chris Blackwell was adamant that if the record made it on its own merits then he would go with it, if not he would cancel our contract. Needless to say, no record could stand on its own without the backing of the recording company so we died. I was begining to feel like Kilroy, just getting to the top of the wall only to slide down again. Hollywood Brown was put away and I went back to being Jon Jon Keefe. I really appreciated the faith my two managers had in me and in time their good taste was repayed as they went on to have a big hit with 'Pass the Dutchie' [Musical Youth].

I had not given up the club because, even with all the talk about fame, there was still a part of me that didn't quite believe it. I had been there many times before, after all. But I had to give up working in the daytime, it was now too much. I bid farewell to another close group of friends and concentrated on finishing my house. I was well aware of the difficulties of working as an agent now and realised that I wasn't cut out to be as hard-nosed as I needed to be. And it had been getting harder and harder to get top name acts to ensure a full house at the club. I would put out request slips on busy nights at the club looking for suggestions from our patrons as to who would ensure their attendance at the club. Even our patrons had no perception of the difficulty we had of booking the acts they suggested. They wanted Morecombe and Wise, The Two Ronnies, Benny Hill and it was difficult to explain to them that these performers were strictly TV artists and never did cabaret. I was always left with a select group of artists sure to fill the club at a price that was ever escalating as their managements knew that without them we had very few alternatives and so their prices went up and we were held over a barrel. I would write guaranteeing that our customers would have a great night out with a three course meal, dancing to bands and the certainty on recommendation that the cabaret act would both surprise and entertain them even if they were not a household name. And I was offering all

Starlight Room Programme

that for £15. I always said that an evening out with your wife at a Chinese or Indian or pukka restaurant could not give the entertainment we were able to supply. As I knew from my own experience, I would take my wife out for a meal, get there at seven thirty, order a drink, sit down to a meal, look around the room at who might be in, look at the menu, order the meal and talk about the kids and

168

other little topics that we may not have exhausted before. The meal would arrive and we would eat and drink in prolonged silence, finish the wine, have coffee and be out in the street getting in the car two hours later. Once we got home we'd have another drink and the wife would go to bed as the old man settled down to watch telly. On the other hand, a night at the club had you arriving at seven thirty, ordering some drinks at the bar to a gentle hubbub. There would be a live band playing some light jazz at a level that enabled you to still carry on a conversation with other customers who you may not have seen for a while. The Maitre D' would escort you to your table and you would order your meal and drinks. Then, to break the ice, you could have a dance before your meal. The meal would come and go and another band would come on stage playing more pop songs and dance tunes. Then the lights would dim at 10.30 and it would be cabaret time. There would be no boring, silent interludes inbetween conversations about family holidays or other trivial things. It was show time. I would come on to introduce special celebrations in the club that night, entertain the people and introduce the top act for the evening. The star for that night, whether they were known to you or not, would come on for an hour and surprise you as to how great they were. At the end of their act, at about midnight, there would still be an hour and a half for you both to dance the rest of the night away in your own company and the company of other people you had met that night. No silences, no pregnant pauses, no big bills. In fact, you would be happy and contented to go home at 1.30am and get to bed together.

I painted this scenario so well to our customers but it fell on deaf ears and, although I could have the services of such great acts as Dave Evans (an incredibly talented entertainer and father of Lee Evans), Norman Collier, Johnny More, David Copperfield, Charlie Smithers, The Dallas Boys, Tony Monopoly, The Brother Lees and many many more, all for the price of £15 with two bands and meal thrown in, no, the customers would prefer to pay £40 to £50 for a household name, many of whom were not very appreciative of them.

The Grass is Greener....

Forever striving to get to the top of the bill was what spurred me and many acts like me on. To hear your name called out and walk on to the stage to the sound of tumultuous applause was the single motivating drive for success. Instead of the noise and partial indifference of walking on unannounced and fighting to gain some attention and respect for your craft from an audience who were only there to see the star of their choice. I know it is necessary to have some nerves when you're standing in the wings waiting to go on, but the extent to which some top of the bills were nervous I found so confusing. The top of the bill had the guarantee that the audience had paid good money to come to see them and in my eyes that ensured that they would walk on to an incredible reception. So that meant that they did not have to spend a large part of their act getting to see if the audience appreciated them. It was evident by the huge round of applause as they walked on that the act was in the company of an audience that sometimes adored them. I even found myself comforting and assuring some top names that the club was packed out and could have been even more so if we had more seats. I always thought they should go out and enjoy the adulation. Plus the fact was that the financial rewards for one night's work were incredible.

It was a different scenario though when I had to present a comeback show for a star who had been some time away from performing. One such star was the exceedingly talented Lena Zavaroni. You may remember Lena was a huge star from a very young age, winning *Opportunity Knocks*. She had an enormous voice for such a young child and the British public took her to their hearts. The stresses and strains of starting so young contributed, I assume, to all the problems she had and her terrible fight against anorexia. This one night Lena was making a comeback starting at The Starlight Club. She had never worked there before and was in a state of nerves that was almost making her sick stage-side. I can honestly say I was never jealous of any artist's good fortune, only ever puzzled at the lack of better fortune for myself. I know I was a kind and friendly entertainer, so I found myself comforting Lena backstage, peering through the curtains, telling her what a fantastic draw she was for the club and assuring her that the audience was thrilled that she was appearing in front of them. She was shaking like a leaf and I kept up a reassuring, gentle conversation of how great she was going to be and that she just to go out on stage and revel in the joy of an audience that loved her. I went out and did my opening spot and introduced her,

'Ladies and Gentlemen, the one and only Miss Lena Zavoroni.' The emaciated figure that walked onto the stage elicited a silent gasp followed by an enormous standing ovation before Lena had said a word or sung a note. It was overwhelming to feel the care and generosity of the crowd. Lena proceeded to do her show and the evening was an enormous success.

Another act who was always a great success at the club was a fantastic young comedy magician called Wayne Dobson. Once again, I was called on to spiritually and physically support a top-of-the bill. As we were about to open the show, Wayne's manager asked if it was possible for me to help Wayne to the centre stage where he would have to do most of his act sitting on a high stool. I agreed and made sure the stage was set to make this happen. The last time Wayne had been at the club, some patrons had thought that he was under the influence of drink or drugs as much of his once impeccable, fast dialogue was rather slurred and difficult to understand. I set the stage and the manager asked how I was going to explain why Wayne had to do the act sitting down. I said I would tell the audience that he had been in a car crash and yet still found the way to fulfil his engagement as this was sure to endear him to them even more. I introduced Wayne, took his arm and helped him to his stool. I came off and stood in the wings and asked God what it would take for me to go on last and earn the kind of money Wayne was getting. The manager saw me peering through the tabs and I asked him what was going on with Wayne. He told me that Wayne had contracted Multiple Sclerosis. I was stunned, looked skyward and asked God to cancel my last request. Wayne had to give up performing not very long after and I heard that he started training other people to do the fabulous conjuring and comedy act that had been so cruelly taken away from him.

So with acts like Lena who died very young, God bless her, and Wayne and many other artists who were or almost were household names, it always seems the grass is always greener. But there are so many interesting stories about the rise and fall of fame and stardom. It seems that though we try to hold the lesson of these cruel incidences in our mind, it never seems long before the old neurosis comes back, asking how do I get on in showbusiness.

25. The Up's and Downs of Performing

The cabaret business was getting harder and harder and there was only a handful of acts who could draw full crowds at the club. That was only one reason why we could not keep the club busy and we were down to three nights a week from January to Easter, full weeks for Easter and back to three nights until the beginning of October when the winter season kicked in and then it was back to seven nights a week. It was imperative to book big stars for the slow weeks when you could guarantee a full house. The only problem was every other cabaret venue had the same policy, so we were all running after the

Jon Jon with Tommy Cooper

services of the biggest stars. This meant that their managements could ask ever-bigger fees, with the booking going to the highest bidder. You hit the jackpot if you could book Tommy Cooper but there was a deal of aggravation involved in booking him. Tommy would arrive at the club for band call with a rather posh sounding lady accompanying him, along with a giant of a man, his son. Chests of props would be brought into the club which had a rather restricted back stage area. I would settle Tommy and his lady companion. Coffee and drinks would be offered and I would go off to help his son to organise his enormous amount of props. Tommy would come out to do his band call. It could be a very difficult time because he was a stickler for the music to be very precise. The backbone of our cabaret show was the superb quality of our cabaret band which boasted some of the finest musicians in the biz. They read the most difficult music at the speed of light. Tommy's music left much to be desired, it was written many years hence on battered pieces of manuscript. There are so many stories from people who came into contact with him and many of those stories came from musicians. A group at one club incurred the wrath of this enormous and sometimes formidable man. He berated them for continually making a hash of some of his backing music, the mere fact that what they were trying to read at breakneck speed were scraps of paper that had seemed once to have been serviettes, and were now crumpled and stained and not really worthy of a top act like Tommy Cooper. He was really harsh on the guys and it was tolerated by the management as musicians came at the bottom of the ladder along with dancers when it came to being appreciated for their expertise. So although they were unable to fight back on this occasion they were determined to get their own back. Along with the vast amount of props, there was a three foot high, four foot wide white wooden gate. Tommy had props littered all around the stage and the gate took pride of place right in the middle. Tommy would do a gag with a prop and then walk up to the gate, open it, and for no apparent reason, walk through it on the way to a prop at the front of the stage. But not this time. It appears that the drummer had put a tack in the gate so that it would not open. Tommy tried a couple of times and was unsuccessful. He could have just walked to the side and walked round it but he was on automatic pilot, had drunk quite a bit of alcohol and he had been walking through the gate to get to the next gag for years, so that when it didn't open he walked off only twenty minutes into his act and never came back.

Back at The Starlight, when he and his companion with the posh voice arrived at the club all was happy and bright but as the show neared, raised voices could be heard from the dressing room and the once dulcet posh tones turned into a high-pitched scream. I didn't hear any of this and personally I was thrilled to be on the same programme with one of my own and the public's comedy greats. I introduced to the people, 'Ladies and Gentlemen, the one and only Mr Tommy Cooper!' He didn't appear. So, another drum roll, and I say again, 'Tommy Cooper!' Nothing. Standing on stage with nothing going on is hell on earth. What I didn't know was that Tommy would not appear when he was introduced and in fact he alone decided when he would walk on stage. The crowd became restless at Tommy's non-appearance and were equally embarrassed at the look of terror on my face. I was always able to ad-lib over most kinds of hiccup but this was different; I just did not know what was supposed to happen. I was rarely lost for words on stage and I was very embarassed. Then, after what seemed an eternity, a drunken voice boomed out from backstage, 'Uh huh! I can't get out. I'm locked in the wardrobe with a large G&T and a Havana and I can't find the light.' Tommy kept this very funny muttering going on for ages as I introduced him again and again. At last he appeared to tumultuous laughter and applause and dismissed me. Everybody enjoyed my crushing embarrassment but me. If I had been told what was going to happen, I would have been more than happy to act as Mr Cooper's stooge. As it was, I was really miffed. I grabbed hold of his enormous son and said, 'If Mr Cooper wants me to be in the act, I want some of his considerable wages.' He brushed me off and told me I needed a sense of humour. I still carry the crushing embarrassment that I felt. But that's showbusiness.

Typical Tommy Cooper Gags

I was in my car, driving along and my boss rang up and he said, 'You've been promoted.' And I swerved. And then he phoned up a second time and said, 'You've been promoted again.' And I swerved again. He rang up a third time and said, 'You're now the managing director.' And I went into a tree. Then a policeman

came up and said, 'What happened to you?' And I said, 'I careered off the road'.

The police arrested two kids yesterday, one was drinking battery acid, the other was eating fireworks. They charged one and let the other one off.

A man takes his dog to the vet. 'My dog's cross-eyed, is there anything you can do for him?' 'Well,' says the vet, 'let's take a look at him.' So he picks the dog up and examines his eyes, then checks his teeth. Finally he says, 'I'm going to have to put him down.' '"What? Because he's cross-eyed?' 'No, because he's really heavy.'

A policeman stopped me and said, 'Would you please blow into this bag, sir?' I said, 'What for, officer?' He said, 'My chips are too hot.'

The worst air disaster in several years occured today when a small two-seater Cessna plane crashed into a cemetary. Search and rescue workers have recovered 1,826 bodies so far and expect that number to climb as digging continues into the night.

I rang a local building firm and said 'I want a skip outside my house.' He said, 'I'm not stopping you.'

'I'm going to cut off your trouser legs and put them in the library.' 'That's a turn up for the books,' I said.

Somebody complimented me on my driving yesterday; they put a note on my windscreen it said, 'Parking fine'

Two cannibals eating a clown. One says, 'Does this taste funny to you?'

26. Where the f--- is the arsehole?

I have spoken of the great highs and lows of showbiz. One of the most crushing disappointments is to have a club of five hundred customers eagerly awaiting an evening's cabaret and having to announce at the last minute that the act they had booked to see would not be appearing. It was not possible to recompense the almost baying audience for the non-appearance of their expected cabaret star and even though we were not responsible for the stars' non-appearances, we were nevertheless left with a situation it was impossible to resolve. Some acts would telephone at the last moment informing us of their non-appearance that evening, which would leave me no time at all to engage the services of whoever was available locally to help me fill the date. There were some stalwarts who would normally come to my aid. And, on the evening after announcing the change in the evening's performance, I invariably had to make up some cock-and-bull story when in fact it came to light later that the act simply could not be bothered to show up. This particular sort of indifference tended to come from some of the recently successful acts made famous on TV.

One act that caused me incredible difficulty was so talented and loved by the public. I had seen him rise from an eager, willing, ready-to-learn, fantastically talented artist and climb right to the top of the tree to vanish to who knows where. I booked him at the club as often as I could even though his fees were really out of our reach. So although we lost on the booking fee we were able to scrape though financially because of the quality of the clientele and the bar receipts that we took. A four night engagement which financially for us was a loss leader turned into a nightmare for me personally. The evening was electric, the customers were in high spirits and were spending bundles of money. The champagne was flowing and expensive cigar smoke filled the air. I eagerly awaited show time as I knew I would be particularly well received because most of the customers were our regular punters. Showtime came but there was no sight of the star. We held off the cabaret time to give us time to clear the room of unwanted glasses and crockery and give us more time to serve drinks. The customers didn't notice the delay and, after half an hour, I needed to go on stage. I had forty minutes to do and drew it out as long as I could, waiting for a sign from the Maitre D' that the act was ready to go on. Coming to the end of my spot, a waiter walked past the front of the stage and as subtle as only waiters can be, slipped me a note reading, 'He isn't here yet. Keep going.'

This guy was being paid £12,000 for a night's work and I was on a pittance in comparison and I was being asked once again to cover the arse of some star who for some reason or other did not or could not care about his contractual duties and his fans. All the front tables were occupied by his formidable fan club. They were all done up to the nines and sporting large bunches of flowers. As my impromptu act got longer and longer, with the help of my incredible backing band, the leader of his fan club started to become agitated at her star's non-appearance thinking that I was trying to steal some of his limelight.

She began miming 'Fuck off' through venomous lips. I carried on regardless and, after over an hour, received the signal that the act was here and was being dressed for his performance. It still took a little time before he was ready and then, as though nothing had happened, he shuffled on stage oblivious to the mayhem he had caused. This happened every night of his run until the fourth night when he was even later than usual. The fan club leader was still abusing me verbally when I got the signal to get the act on. As I did, I called the fan club leader to the stage pretending to make reference to the crowd of her standing. As she walked, smiling to the stage, I grabbed her and asked her to read aloud over the microphone the messages I had been receiving. She read the waiter's note, 'We don't know where the fuck this arsehole is. Please do your best to keep going.' The band, the waiters and some of the customers who knew what had been happening, cheered. I left the stage and bumped straight into the act who, when I first knew him made Robert Redford look plain, but who now was managing to do a fantastic impression of Harold Steptoe. I had worked all my professional life at trying to be as artistically good as I possibly could. But on this particular night I learned what I had been lacking all the time: vulnerability. As the star shuffled on hardly knowing where he was, the crowd gave him a standing ovation just for showing up. Needless to say, he stormed the show once again and I learned another trick from showbiz.

27. Back to Benny in a Dress & High Heels

That thing happened again: a phone call right out of the blue. It was Dennis Kirkland, the director of The Benny Hill Show. 'J.J., dear boy, how are you fixed? Ben asked me to ask you to come back on the show. If you're up for it, get your arse to Teddington Studios 8 a.m. Monday.'

I hardly had time to ask how or why before he was gone. We hadn't discussed salary or anything else; I would have done it for nothing anyway but never let on. I had watched a succession of artists take my place and seen them last for a few shows before being replaced by someone new. I assume they, like me, were never told why they were being replaced - you just turned on the TV one day and saw someone else doing what you used to do. No reasons or explanations, that was it. I was excited beyond belief and shared the news with my family. My dear wife knew how

It's the 'lovely' Jon Jon!

much it meant to me to be on a major TV show again and the trials and tribulations of the goings on at the club became secondary. It was a tremendous financial boost as I was still able to do the TV in the daytime and rush off to the club at night.

I got to the studios early, had breakfast and renewed my acquaintances with props men, sparks, cameramen, wardrobe, make-up, in fact every one that matters for you to be accepted not just as a good actor but a nice person.

I walked down the corridor to my dressing room as Dennis was coming out of Benny's room. 'Hello Den, me son.'

'J.J., great to see you.'

Now I'm six feet tall and Dennis was about five foot four, I put my arms around his shoulder and said, 'Dennis, in all honesty, was it something I said?'

Dennis, although a director, was the master of the understatement and, without flinching, he said what he always said when he wanted to get his own back on me, 'Go see Allard in wardrobe and put on a dress and high heels.'

So it was that I got back on the show. I thanked God and thought I had died and gone to heaven.

The first person I bumped into was dressed in exactly the same costume as me: a crumpled dress, pinefore, crinkly stockings and curler-hair wig. It was Toddy.

'Have you upset Dennis too?' I said.

'Jon Jon, dear boy. How the hell are you? And where have you been? Are you back for a while? What has occurred?'

'To all of your questions, the answer is - yes and why the

uniform?"

'Lack of dialogue ,dear boy. And diminishing brain cells.'

Thames TV was by far the best station in terms of viewing figures for comedy shows. They had Benny Hill, Morecambe and Wise, Tommy Cooper, Jim Davidson and Des O'Connor. With a staff of two thousand people, it was a wonderful place to work. The head of Light Entertainment was Phillip Jones, a dapper, charming, bespoke-suited lovely man. He would show his face on the floor of the studio checking with Ben and Den that all was well. Benny included Phillips' name as the tag to many sketches, and, when lost for a tag,

Jon Jon enjoying prison life with Benny Hill [Photo: courtesy of Thames TV]

Ben would look in exasperation off-camera, dressed as a cowboy or a chinaman and, with a brief pause cry, 'Phirrip!' and walk off stage left.

Several years had passed but it was as though I had never been away. I managed to ask seriously not why I had had the push but what had prompted my return. Dennis said the vagaries of showbiz have no sense or rhyme or reason attached to them. It was just that he and Ben were in

185

the rushes studio looking at some old sketches when I appeared and Ben said, 'You know Den, Jon Jon had a much broader range of characters and was so useful in the musical numbers I think we should get him back again.' So something as simple as that gave me a career boost again.

The depths to which grown men would stoop to make a living were evident when I would see a revered professional actor like Henry McGee dressed in the most outlandish costumes. Toddy and I asked him what he had done to upset Dennis as he came from wardrobe dressed in a forties floral print dress, an apron, a really terrible wig and excruciatingly high-heeled shoes. Henry was teetotal, smoked a pipe and had the driest sense of humour: 'I heard the word "residual" being bandied about and knew what the next sketch was going to be. Seeing as I was not scheduled to be in it, my gut instinct told me to go put on a dress as I was bound to be thrown in it by our beloved director just because I look so damn awful.' Invariably it worked more times than not. If we didn't end up in the sketch, we three always raised a few laughs. Henry McGee had a pedigree of fine, straight acting performances. He was also the finest straight man to many of the country's comics: Benny Hill, Charlie Drake, Tommy Cooper, Frankie Howerd, Terry Scott, Jimmy Tarbuck, Reg Varney, Dick Emery and Eric Sykes. It seems that Henry's only ambition was to be an old actor. It is impossible to explain the importance of Henry's role as straight man. He had to be word perfect and serve up Ben's lines so that Ben could feel safe in playing with his own dialogue. It was imperative that he felt safe because the sketches that had all the dialogue in were shot in front of an audience.

There has been so much written about Benny's rise through variety and his ground-breaking work in the early days of TV comedy. It was surprising to see how he was almost petrified of appearing in front of an audience. He was most at home writing, producing and filming the major parts of the show, but come studio days filming in front of an audience he became a bundle of nerves. In all the years I worked with Benny, I never heard him lose his temper. He had his own way of showing disaproval: he would gently hum or whistle and bite his fingernails. His nerves on a studio day would have him biting his nails down to the quick to the point where he had to have plasters put over his nails and made up. I sometimes had to have my hand used for a close-up instead of his.

28. Benny – The Inside Story

I don't think anybody really got to know Benny properly. He was a really nice, private man. The show was his total reason for living. If he wasn't appearing on it, he was always thinking of sketches and working on things in preparation for the next show. If he wasn't working on the show, he very rarely did any other perfoming. Occasionally he would accept a commercial if it was shot out of the country. One such occasion was for a beer commercial that was to be shot in Greece. Benny loved the Mediterranean and any excuse to be paid to go there, he jumped at. For this particular job it was a two day shoot in Greece. Benny said he would like to do it but he would need to be flown there two days before shooting began. Invariably the company making the commercial would agree and then having nicked two more days abroad, he would add that an old performer like him might need two days to get over it once the commercial was completed. Without talking about money, he usually managed to get a week away in the sun. He would not waste the extra days. His joy was to sit at the back of some seafront cafe watching the comings and goings of the tourists and the local people. He would write sketches on serviettes and an old notepad, watching waiters and customers and the interaction between the two. I ended up playing many of the characters from those working holidays away. Benny loved languages and was very efficient at communicating in Spanish, German and French. He was also a good musician, as many of the sketches showed. Many of his sketches had a continental theme to them.

Benny never made waves about money for he never seemed bothered about it. He was known locally by the shopkeepers around Queensgate where he lived for many years and Teddington where he finally ended his days. The studio was almost embarrassed by his not wanting to be driven to the studios. Benny had never learned to drive officially but one of his great joys was to drive himself around the lot in any car, motorcycle or other piece of mechanical equipment that we might be using for the show. His face was a picture to behold as he pottered about between set-ups. The reason he refused taxi rides from Queensway to Teddington was that it gave him the opportunity to go on the underground and study the actions of people on the train. He would go to his local shop and buy his shopping, mainly yoghurts and fruits, for his working day at the studio. Benny only had one kidney and when he was not working he relaxed quite heavily and he loved his food and a glass of wine. He was prone to put on a lot of weight when not working and he was very severe with himself when it was time to go back to work. It was said that this heavy see-sawing effect on his kidney had a great deal to do with his death. So, Benny would be set out with a plastic bag with all his goodies in it and he would get on the train and study his eventual victims. On reaching Teddington station, it was about a mile's walk to the studios. Other artists would drive past Benny in their Rollers and Jaguars, and they would always wonder if Ben was hard up, seeing him marching to the studios in the rain.

The *TV Times* wanted to do a colour spread about him in their magazine. He refused point blank. After much persuading he eventually changed his mind and they went to his flat to work out a plan of action. Benny's flat was in a very nice place in Queensgate. But inside it was like stepping back into the fifties. Pride of place was the biggest television it was possible to have and video recorders and tape machines. Also pride of place was a bow-fronted veneered radiogram with curled pictures of his family and of a presentation to the Queen. Apart from the upholstered chair plumb in front of the TV, all the rest had seen better days. The bedroom and bathroom were also furnished from a time long past. The *TV Times* said they could not possibly photograph the flat in its present condition and set about redecorating and refurnishing it. They finished the shoot and Benny insisted they took away all the new furniture and replace it with his original stuff. Dennis Kirkland said he went to Benny's flat one day and there behind the door was a big pile of twenty and fifty pound notes in plastic wrappers from the bank unopened, he said there must have been thousands of pounds there. It seemed he cared not a fig for possessions and wealth. He let his manager and agent worry about the money side of things.

High Budgets with Low Pay

Benny was pleasantly eccentric and was cared for by all his cast and crew. He never appeared to make any outlandish requests for his own needs, but he made sure that the financial needs for the budget for the show were never interfered with. The budget for the show was very high. On location one day I counted one hundred people in the cast and crew. The artists' salaries were not that great, hence the importance of the residuals. Each time I write that word it sends a shiver of anticipation down my spine. To awaken one morning long after the show had gone out and have the postman drop a letter on the mat with a residual cheque in it was the best feeling. I would kiss it and say, thanks Ben.

But, despite the low pay, people would give up the opportunity to work on programmes that paid more money because it was so much fun. The whole atmosphere on the show was of one big happy family. The whole show was driven by the friendship between Dennis and Benny. Benny trusted Dennis implicitly and always said that he was not only the best director Ben had worked with but had become Ben's best friend. Dennis was a powerhouse of inventive ideas and a comic genius. A typical show began by ensuring that Toddy was booked into an hotel or bed and breakfast that had a bar, close as possible to the site we were going to shoot all the running-about bits. Dennis needed to know where Toddy was at all times because he would need to throw him into sketches at the drop of a hat. Toddy's dresser had the monumental task of keeping Toddy supplied with a generous libation at all times so that Toddy never went off looking for some himself. This was because once when Toddy had been appearing at The Palladium with Tommy Steele, he had a good drink and walked out of theatre and disappeared for a couple of days. He turned up drinking Guiness in a pub in Dublin, with no recollection of how he got there. He also appeared in a show in London with Spike Milligan, who was a crazy man, and Valentine Dyall, an old character actor who played the 'Man in Black' on radio many years ago and was a consummate gambler. The production was hilarious anyway, so with the addition of a serious toper and a nutty gambler, nobody knew what would happen in the show from night to night. The show was called *Son of Oblamov*. At one point in the show Spike Milligan was in a coffin on a trestle and the coffin had a half flip lid that allowed Spike to sit up and deliver a line. Unbeknown to him, Toddy had put a couple of tacks in the lid so, upon Spike trying to sit up, the audience were greeted with a loud thud and screaming Goon noises coming from this coffin teetering on this plinthe. Of course the audience went mad.

So, with the executive producer Mr Nigel Cooke having found the perfect site with all the neccessary needs as far as Toddy was concerned, we began several weeks of running around in the depths of winter pretending it was summertime. Dennis and I would turn up at Toddy's lodgings at about 7.45 a.m. Toddy would already be at the bar drinking vodka and orange juice and, as we walked through the door, two drinks of the same would be handed to us as we hit the bar.

'Good morning and heartfelt salutations, O director and fellow thespian,' Todd would greet us.

'Good morning, Mr Todd. A fine night's libation no doubt?'

'Of course, dear chap. Unsurpassed revelry and a good time was had by all.'

Imparting to all and sundry the machinations and tribulations of being an actor., we would have a couple of doubles and get our orders for the day.

'Do we wear dresses today Den?'

'Not today, chaps, parking meter attendants.'

As we left to get in the car, peppermints would be handed out to cover the possibility of the vodka still hanging on our breaths. We didn't want Ben to know that we had been drinking already but I'm sure he was aware of the constant smell of peppermint wafting around the set. One day there had been a run on the peppermint stocks and there were none left. Luckily Todd had a scented throat spray as a back-up and he took two shots and passed it to Dennis. Dennis took two shots and nearly passed out. Apparently Toddy was having it made up with a vodka base. Amidst this hard drinking, serious work was taking place and we were all called upon to do some outrageous stunts for men of our age. Nobody refused a request to jump, be pushed or fall off things – it was all par for the course. Even little Jackie Wright, the man whose head Benny slapped, would be called on at seventy years of age to do some crazy things. Jackie's story reads like something out of a film too. He had been an old variety performer in Northern Ireland and could play trombone, harmonica and sing and tap dance. He had been booked to be in a restaurant crowd scene in the studio and at the rushes Ben saw his potential and thought he could use him as a featured character. In fact, he became so famous that just before he died he had been lined up for a major part in a film in Hollywood. Old habits die hard and Jackie was always looking for a constant supply of tea and cigarettes and apples. Even though he had a supply of apples in his caravan, he wandered into an orchard on location one day and scrumped some apples. He ate them and got the terrible squits and held up shooting his scenes for that day. It turned out they were crab apples. There we were, all dressed in togas for a Roman scene, laurel wreathes on our heads, sandals, the whole bit, and centrestage stands Jackie with Ben about to deliver a line.

Dennis said, 'Action! Go Jackie,'

And Jackie started in a broad Northern Irish brogue, 'Do you know the way to Pompeii, Centurian?'

'Barracks Senator,' came the reply.

Before we could get to the punch line, Dennis would cry, 'Cut! Cut! Would somebody please explain to me that spiral of cigarette smoke billowing from the little Senator's toga?' Jackie always had a cigarette on the go behind his back, ready to have a puff as soon as we had finished the take. 'And would somebody from the wardrobe department please tell me when Roman Senators started wearing horn rimmed glasses.'

Once again Benny had shown how intelligent he had been to take Jackie onto his regular team and how generous and appreciative he was even though he made a career out of slapping this old man's head. Jackie loved it. But when Jackie died Ben needed to replace him with another little old man. First one he tried was a warm-hearted little man called Len. He was a great old pro and had some fantastic stories, but it just didn't work. He used to get letters from viewers complaining about Ben hitting this lovely little old man. Next man he tried was an incredible old performer, without a lie he could do a back flip at seventy years of age. He had owned a tumbling act that worked all the casinos in Las Vegas doing somersaults, cartwheels, back flips and all kinds of acrobatic feats. One the first day of rehearsals, the door opened and Johnny Hutch walked the full length of the rehearsal room on his hands, came out of the handstand with a flip and introduced himself to Ben. He got the job.

Nigel Cooke's brief was to find suitable locations for all the running-around bits and sometime he needed to have buildings to double as manor houses and outbuildings. One location was an ICI conference centre somewhere off the M3. The centre was just hundreds of yards from a village perched on the side of the A3 (or it could have been the A30 or A303 – I can't remember which because I always travelled there in the dark of a November morning and usually drove home inebriated). Anyway, this location had a series of small terraced houses, a few small shops and a lot of pubs for such a small street.

Locating near a Bar

Nigel's brief was also to find suitable accommodation for Bob Todd, which meant it had to have a bar. The sleeping quarters needed to be homely and comfortable, not lavish and snooty, and it had to be within walking distance of the site we were filming on. Dennis and everybody else included in getting Toddy dressed, made up and in some fit state to perform, had to know where to find Toddy all of the time. He was a prime performer on the show and could always be relied upon to be or do something funny. The last pub in the village was only chosen because it was the nearest to the site. I learned a lesson in not making too many plans in show business as finance and practicality are as important, if not more so, than sheer talent. The pub in question had been taken over by a young couple and was not really up to the quality of the other more established pubs in the village. The couple were working on a shoestring budget and could not believe their luck when Nigel plumped for their establishment to house the great Bob Todd. He was duly ensconced and from the off the bar till began to ring out.

On a TV or film set one of the great requirements is the catering. On a cold November morning, having been made up and dressed in a skimpy loin cloth, it was necessary to kick start your heart with at least a bacon sarnie. Lunch came and was well catered for and then we would nip over to see Toddy propped up at the bar regaling all and sundry with his tales of derring-do. Toddy never ate a great deal, as I recall. At the end of the day, prior to going home, we would bid Toddy *adieu* with another quick snifter. And then we would leave him in the wilds of Surrey to entertain the locals as we got on the coach back to Thames TV at Teddington with Dennis to look at the day's rushes. The cameraman was a top-flight guy called Ted Adcock and he said he had done a stint filming the war in Vietnam but you needed much more stamina to shoot a Benny Hill show.

The outcome of three weeks filming at the end of Bob Todd's stay at this young couple's hostelry was that they were almost able to pay off their mortgage. It had been a particularly happy three weeks and Ben, generous to a fault, gave some money to throw a wrap party before we left. Technical support workers, wardrobe, make-up artists, actors and stars, we all had a whale of a send off and the young couple waved us goodbye with tears in their eyes.

Benny never joined in with all these goings-on but must have been well aware of the things we all got up to. But as long as you did your job well and dedicated yourself to help him get the very best out of the show, he was happy. As well as being kind, unassuming and generous.

After a shoot, I usually ended up in something pink -shirts, jerseys, jumpers and leather jackets, all too small for me. I talked this over with the wardrobe master, Allard Tobin, a blond bunch of loveliness himself, asking him why pink and why just too small? He told me I was breaking them in for Mr Kirkland at the end of the shoot.

I asked one of the girls for a gag what they thought of Dennis Kirkland as a director and an all-round human being. The girls said they thought he was a bit flakey This gave me ammunition for another gag to pull on him. On the way to the studios, I stopped off at a sweet shop and bought twelve Cadbury's Flake bars. Then I got the manager of the pub we had breaks in, to rewrite the lunch menu to read, Egg, Flake and chips, Cheese and Flakes on toast, Steak, Flake and chips, and so on, right through the menu. I waited for Den to come in to the pub and I ordered him his usual drink, vodka and orange. The barmaid pulled up the glass and in the bottom of the glass were some cornflakes. Den didn't say a word. The barmaid proceeded to pour the vodka and orange on top of the flakes and Den nonchalantly pressed it to his lips and drank it. He didn't say a word until he had finished the drink, when he casually brought it to the barmaid's attention that there appeared to be something in his drink. The barmaid apologised and gave him another glass. Dennis was the champion of underplaying a gag. We carried on talking about what the day would bring as though nothing had happened.

When we got back to the studios, they were marking out a big Spanish scene. Dennis left the floor and I took the chance of giving all the Hill's Angels a Cadbury Flake bar and asked them on my signal to all march up to him, give him the Flake bar and say, 'Thank you Mr Kirkland but no thanks.' Dennis came back on the floor and I gave the girls the signal. As one, they marched up to him and gave him the bars then walked away. I was hiding behind the studio seats set out for the audience. Dennis paused and shouted, 'Keefe, you are a dead man!' That gag almost cost me my health as I nearly got pneumonia as Dennis kept me in swimming trunks, in, on or under freezing cold water all day. Every day at work was a joy.

I was still running *The Starlight Club* and still having the greatest difficulty in booking great acts to perform there. One of the best was Billy Eckstine. I was a life-long fan of this fantastic singer. I was

overawed at presenting him on stage and I would show my admiration by introducing him with an impression of him and eight bars of his most famous song 'I Apologise'. Next night his beautiful daughter asked me kindly if I wouldn't do it again as her father said I was beginning to sound more like him than himself. Only I

Jon Jon & Billy Eckstine

went and did it again without thinking, only out of sheer admiration. They showed their class by not being cross at what I did. Billy Eckstine was followed up by Jack Jones, an incredible singer but a very tetchy man. We also had Gene Pitney, Billy Daniels and Martha Reeves and the Vandellas.

We did a special charity show for the family of PC Blakelock who had died in the Tottenham riots. We invited The Right

Douglas Hurd & Jon Jon

Honourable Home Secretary, Douglas Hurd, and his wife and distinguished guests. Mr Hurd had agreed to squeeze us in for a brief appearance from his very busy schedual. The police sniffer dogs were sent in first and when all was clear we were informed that he would stay for about thirty minutes. The cabaret consisted of many acts: Mike Reid, The Brotherhood of Man, Charlie Smithers and several more. Nicholas Parsons and I did an auction and we raised many thousands of pounds. Mr Hurd and his wife stayed much longer than their allotted time and said they hadn't enjoyed themselves so much for years.

Another poitical figure who visted the club as guest of honour and speaker for the North of London Conservative Party was Mr John Major. Mr Major was always portrayed as a very grey and bland personality, but he was a revelation on the night he came to the club. My thoughts are that if he had displayed as much humour in his parliamentary career as he showed on this night he would have been more highly regarded. He told us a great joke: As it was coming up to Christmas, there was a huge amount of mail that Mount Pleasant Post Office had to deal with for Father Christmas. A ballot was taken and one postman was delegated to a spot in the post office to deal with all the Santa postcards. He was inundated, but one particular card touched his heart. 'Dear Santa,' it read, 'I am a widower as my dear wife recently passed away and has left me to bring up three children under nine. The struggle to do this is terrible but I am trying to cope as best I can. We are living on subsistance and now Christmas is here I don't know how I am going to buy presents for my three

Jon Jon, Ross McWhirter & John Major

beautiful children. Could you please see your way clear to sending me £50 so that I can put a smile on my small children's faces?'; The acting Santa was so touched by this heartfelt request that he took it around the sorting office and showed it to his mates. Post Office workers were in litigation with their bosses themselves at this time but they managed to scrape together £25 to send to the bereaved family. A week later the acting Santa opened a reply to his donation: 'Dear

Father Christmas. Thank you for the £25 you sent me, but I think the thieving bastards at the Post Office stole the other 25 quid.'

Benny's Weight Problem

Mr Don Taffner had done a fantastic job of selling The Benny Hill Show in America. Under his auspices we went back into production as if we had never been away. The whole crew was re-formed and we went back into rehearsals. Ben had put on a great deal of weight while he wasn't working, he used food and drink as a comforter, so he had to go on another crash diet. As with everything else to do with the show, once he made his mind up he was extremely determined and the weight just fell off. But it was getting harder and harder as he got older. His love of food was brought to my attention one day at lunch by Henry McGee. John Mortimer, the famous writer and playwrite, was visiting the rehearsal room in Kingston-upon-Thames and was delighted at the lycra-clad dancing ladies. He was a great fan of Benny's and they got on like a house on fire. We broke for lunch and Ben ordered a steak and chips and peas. Henry said he hadn't noticed it before but Ben proceeded to eat all the peas in one go, then all the chips and then the steak, taking care not to mix any of the three things on the plate together. He would always follow his main course with a big helping of ice cream and some red wine. As with all people with weight problems, the guilt would set in and it would be back to his yoghurts and fruit for the rest of the day.

Ben and I shared the same birthday: 21 January. On that day, half way through morning rehearsals, Ted Taylor, Ben's fantastic rehearsal pianist, would play an arpeggio on the piano and the door would open and a birthday cake would be brought into the rehearsal room. We would all gather around and sing 'Happy Birthday' to

Benny. Meanwhile Dennis would have made arrangements for a much smaller cake to be put behind some scenery to be given to me by Den's production girls Angie Carter, Fizz Walters and Auriol Lee. As the rest of the cast were singing

**Jon Jon & Benny sharing
the same birthday**

'Happy birthday Ben', the three girls would be whispering to me, "'appy birthday J.J.' The rest of the day had been set aside for us all to celebrate Ben's birthday at a local restaurant where arrangements were made for a wonderful meal with lashings of champagne – all paid for by Benny. He was always very generous and spared no expense to have a great time on his birthday with people whom he considered his family.

Practical Jokers

The three production ladies were cherished by Ben and Den. In their capacity as PA, they were responsible for property, scripts and floor management and for generally making things happen. They took no truck from Dennis in his sometimes outrageous requests. They were more than his equal and their banter was first class. They were also capable of pulling the wool over all the men's eyes. One particular trick they played on me frightened the life out of me. The outside running around bits were hard and tiring and the weather was never very kind as we always filmed in the winter at Thorpe Park while it was closed for the season. One very tough day had me in a swimming suit in the depths of winter pretending it was summer again. It was neccessary to have some alcohol to drink during the day to act as an anti-freeze if nothing else. We drove back from Thorpe Park to the studios at Teddington to watch the rushes of the work that had been shot that day. Dennis, Angie and Fizz got into Den's famous old beaten-up Cortina Estate. It was famous on the lot because it was full of props and scripts and all kinds of pink apparel, Den's colour of choice. I got into my car and set off back to the studio ahead of their car. A few miles down the road there was a crackle and a hiss and a voice said, 'Oscar Victor, come in. We have just seen a car weaving across the central white line. We think the driver could have been drinking. Please stop and apprehend. The registration number is...' I was puzzled because my radio wasn't on and yet I could hear this police message. 'The car is a yellow Citroen, registration number...' They repeated the message again and then it dawned on me I was driving my wife's car – a yellow Citroen. I went into a blind panic, winding down the window, sticking my head out and gulping in huge gasps of air. My life flashed before my eyes and I wondered how I would be able to carry on without a driving licence. I was mortified. I checked my lights and speed limit and gingerly drove as carefully as I could while the message continued to come over the radio. I managed to get back to the studios without being stopped and sat in the car park waiting for the others to turn up while thanking God at my incredible good fortune. As I was about to get out of the car, a voice came over the radio again and said, 'Mr Keefe, remember that we have so many means at our disposal for keeping sometimes lippy actors in their place. Able Charlie Victor over and out.' Fizz Walters had been working on *The Bill* cop show, and knew all the pukka call signs. It turned out that she had hidden a police walkie-talkie under the front seat of my car. Things like that happened to me all the time. A cameraman called Ted Adcock said at the end of filming he was going back to Vietnam for a rest.

The show was a resounding success in America playing on hundreds of TV stations sometimes twice a day. The future was guaranteed as long as the Americans loved the show. They said that Benny had brought burlesque back to the States and a long line of entertainers were lining up to applaud him and maybe make a cameo appearance on the show: Burt Reynolds, Clint Eastwood, Phyllis Diller and many more. Benny was happy again and was working harder than ever. We were still shooting the show at Teddington Studios It was now being used as a production facility as the show was being represented by the Don Taffner Organisation for Thames

International and Don seemed as happy as it was possible to be with the arrangement.

Thames TV at Teddington was a small intimate location with a wonderful atmosphere. Next door was a pub called *The Anglers* where many a new idea or format was invented over several jars of ale. From morning to night the pub had stars, technicians, staff and management coming and going and the place would be alive with laughter. The best place for an artist to be would be the restaurant in Thames TV on a shooting day. The restaurant could have three or four casts of different shows in for lunch. There was cast and crew from The Morecombe and Wise Show, Eric and Ernie and their crew, the Des O'Connor Show and crew, Tommy Cooper and crew, and of course

The Benny Hill Show. The atmosphere in the room was electric. The laughter and ribaldry was fantastic and I felt privileged to be a part of it. The noise of laughter was incredible, each show seeming to out do the others for fun and

Dennis Kirkland, Jon Jon & Bob Todd with Pig!

laughter. Above all the laughter was one voice skitting from table to table getting the loudest laughs, a little ginger-headed nutter known to all the stars and staff for his non-stop humour: director Dennis Kirkland. Den was known to all as a cheeky ribald funster and left no stone unturned in pursuit of a laugh. Dennis, Henry and I were in the bar waiting to go in to lunch one day, gagging away over a vodka and orange, with Henry drinking a soft drink and pulling pensively on his pipe. Across a crowded bar a well-known booming theatrical voice said, 'Henry, old chap, are you still appearing on that scruffy comic show?' Henry drew the pipe from his mouth, paused, and said, 'Yes, and I've just bought myself a Cessna.' Dennis, Henry and I broke out in three-part harmony singing 'Residuals' and the bar broke into laughter.

Days filled with Laughter

I was fortunate enough to have been in some of Ben's great sketches. One of them was 'The Halitosis Kid'. Ben dressed as a cowboy and everything that he breathed on fainted or bent away from his breath until he met a fair maiden whose sense of smell was shot and they skipped off happily together. This was the set-up for a whole series of cowboy gags as so we had to build a Wild West town set at Thorpe Park. A whole main street was erected and lots of scenes were played out. In one, Henry McGee was cast as Dirty Jake, a top-to-toe black-clad villain. Dennis pulled a stroke on Henry that included all the members of the cast and crew. Henry was on a platform twenty feet above the saloon bar awaiting the arrival of the hero, Ben. Henry had Ben's lady in his grasp and Ben had to shoot Henry to gain her freedom. At rehearsal Dennis had Henry on the platform and was lining up the shot and, for rehearsal's sake without Ben being there, upon a gunshot Henry was to fall and keep his legs up in the air until Dennis shouted, 'Cut!' Dennis said it might take a while and asked Henry to bear with him. Dennis called, 'Action!', there was a gunshot and Henry fell out of view except for his legs and boots showing above the balustrade. As soon as Henry fell, Dennis got the whole cast and crew to hide behind any piece of scenery there was. Henry lay there for ages and ages without flinching, his aging legs not faultering for a moment. Then, after some great time, his professionalism got the better of him and he gingerly arose to a bare street and cautiously asked, 'Was that alright for you, Mr ZANUCK?'

**Jon Jon playing
The Gay Cabellero**

An old Hollywood tag line. Everybody appeared clapping and laughing at Henry's undoubted professionalism.

I spent a good deal of time dressed as a camp cowboy. I rode into this scene on a very fey horse, dismounted and, before gingerly mounting the steps to the saloon, putting a horse bag on my horse with the word *Harrods* embroidered on it. My next foray was in a vivid pink cowboy suit, gloves, hat, boots, everything, and cast as the Gay

208

Cabellero. I would be subjected to day-long jibes about my typecasting and my undoubted fondness for my uniform. The crew were the most taunting. 'Hello Cowboy!' they would cry. 'Could you kill a man...?'

Eventually I would lisp, 'How do you get into those tight pink jeans?'

'Well, you could start with a gin and tonic,' the reply would come. And so it went on, every day hard work and long hours but filled with laughter.

29. All My Mates Began to Die

With the famous words, time and tide wait for no man, members of the crew began to die. Little Jackie Wright was the first at the age of eighty-three. He had left the show years before through ill-health but Ben had plenty of unseen sketches with him in them so he would have Dennis include them into more recent shows so that Jackie would not feel left out. Next was a great unsung hero, Ted Taylor, Benny's rehearsal pianist. He was a fabulous piano player and really tuned in to Ben's musical requests. Ben relied a great deal on music right through the show and it was Ted's main task to supply it.

Ted Taylor's funeral was one of the hippest funerals we had ever been to. Being Jewish it was celebrated in a great way with a request from his family for it not be too sombre. We went back to his recording studio in south London where a marquee had been erected behind the studio. Ted's musical ability had spread right through all facets of the business and the attendance at his funeral showed this: there were actors, jazz men, film people and recording artists all there to show their respects. The atmosphere in the marquee was electric as people who had not met up for years told stories of times spent with Ted or in productions with each other. Cynicism is the order of the day when musicians get together and the stories are always caustic and funny. The *pièce de resistance* was Ted's grand piano. It was placed centre of the marquee with a large sign on. It was his parting shot and it read, 'If at first you don't succeed, lower your standards.' This evoked a huge round of laughter and applause from all who came across it.

Showbiz is the cruellest World

Ben was always so saddened by young comics deprecating his shows. He would come to rehearsals having seen the likes of Ben Elton slay him on TV and he always wondered why. He knew how difficult it was to make people laugh and totally supported any way of doing it – old school or the new alternative way. Ben had nothing but good things to say about other artists, knowing how difficult comedy is. One time in particular he was most distressed at a show about Lenny Henry trying to break into the American comedy scene. Lenny was most disparaging when asked about Benny's fantastic success in America, 'How the Americans could find this old comed funny is completely beyond me,' he said. He was then shown doing a spot in a comedy club in America where he totally degraded a woman asking if she had ever had any Jamaican in her. So much for sexism and dirty old men. Benny was really sad that Lenny had been so down on him for Ben thought Lenny was a really good comic.

When Ben was sacked by Thames TV it broke his heart. Especially as he was Thames' most prolific earner. He was unable to comprehend how Thames could consider firing him as he was earning more money for them than anyone else. His shows were still being shown in a hundred countries around the world, America was still clamouring for more shows and it just made no sense. Phillip Jones was no longer head of Light Entertainment and each one hour show was costing more and more. A man called John Howard Davies took control of Light Entertainment and had decided on a new programme policy. It appears that it was possible to produce three or four programmes for the price of one Benny Hill show and, what with political correctness, and the chance of not acquiring another franchise at Thames, even though Benny was the most successful comedian at that time in the world, his show was cancelled. No great show of thanks and appreciation, just a time in the not too distant future for the show to come to an end. Ben, Dennis and the cast and crew were shattered.

Fortunately I was still a director at The Starlight but Dennis went from being the most successful director of the biggest comedy TV show in the world to having to draw the dole. Showbusiness is the cruellest world because people's misconceptions are that while you are working in, or appearing on TV you must be earning a fortune. In fact, only the leading names are the ones who are earning the bulk of the money.

It wasn't just losing a salary that hurt me, it was the prospect of not working with all the people that I had spent sixteen working years of my life with. I was fortunate that I had a family and my life was full, but many people in the biz dedicate their whole life to entertaining whilst making little provision for any mishap that may occur. Even the biggest names can have the carpet pulled out from under them whilst still having to appear to be living the high life with all the expenses that incurred, and often having to pay taxes and expenses for money earned while they were no longer employed. Oft-times we pose the question, 'Whatever happened to...?' Many times well-known artists died alone and broke.

Benny is Struck Down

The show was cancelled and we all went our separate ways. Dennis spent a long time on the dole, applying for all kinds of jobs as a producer or director or other less notable jobs in TV – anything to get back to work. He would apply for positions and, when they read his CV, fresh-faced employers would say he was over-qualified for the job. Then one day I got a call from Dennis saying that Carlton TV were going to take up the show again. Dennis said Benny was all set up and all the old cast and crew were being lined up. Ben was about to sign the contract when he had a minor stroke.

The series of events that followed were broadcast worldwide. Ben was struck down again with a bigger heart attack and was admitted to the Royal Brompton Hospital. Dennis took control of his friend Benny's life and communicated his condition to the world. Ben kept up a brave front while being very ill, still laughing and joking with doctors and nurses. One day, out of the blue, he was visited by his greatest admirer, Michael Jackson. Ben was as thrilled to meet Michael as Michael was to meet Ben and they spoke of plans to do a TV show together. Ben was released from hospital and went back to his apartment in Teddington. Dennis was constantly in touch with him, going around to see him or phoning every day. Then Dennis phoned over a weekend and got no reply. Ben had told him only recently how much better he was feeling and that he was having some great ideas and he was writing for the new shows. Dennis knew that he had been taking short walks so he thought that he just kept missing him. He became rather concerned when he still couldn't reach Ben so he went around to his flat. He knocked on the door but didn't get a reply so he borrowed a ladder to get over the balcony. Once on the balcony, he could see his dear friend plotted up infront of his two TV sets and video recorder, a plate of food and a bottle of wine by his side. Den could see that Benny was dead. He called over the balcony to a neighbour to call the police and smiled at the thought that Ben had passed peacefully away doing what he loved the most – watching TV, looking for new ideas, enjoying his food and a bottle of wine.

The police came and broke into the apartment and let Dennis in. Dennis said Ben's greatest fear was to be stricken down and unable to move but still having the mental capacity to think of great comedy ideas. He had asked Den to shoot him if it ever came to that. Dennis was happy not to have to do anything more than straighten Ben's fantastic mop of hair and close his eyes.

Benny Dies – a very rich man

Benny died a very, very rich man even though he never at any time showed that he cared for money or wealth. He said you could only wear one suit at a time and he never needed anything except the finances to create what he loved the best, writing and performing on TV. Dennis, along with Ben's agents, had to go through the contents of Ben's apartment to straighten up his affairs. Ben said he had made a will in 1961 leaving all his money to his family. They had all died before him so it would all go to his next of kin - nieces and nephews he had never met. Dennis had encouraged him to update the will as he had become an extremely wealthy man. It seems that Ben never got around to it save to say that Dennis found a scrap of paper in his flat with a list of names on it leaving £2,000,000 to be divided up between them. Unfortunately he had not signed it. I asked Den if his name was on it and he said, 'Yes.' I gingerly asked him if my name was on it and he said, 'Yes.' Once again, I was so near yet so far away. As disappointed as we both were, we agreed that no amount of money could have made up for the love, joy and laughter we had shared with this nice man over many years.

Ben died on Saturday, 18 April, 1992 and was buried shortly after in Southampton. We filed out of the church behind the coffin and the clouds opened with hail, rain and snow and we were all soaked. Dennis said Benny was having a joke on us right up to the end. He also said that if Benny could have had his own way he would have got Dennis to reverse print the funeral and instead of being buried he and we would have all ended up back in the pub.

30. Trouble at The Starlight

I was still fighting with a pig of a club owner who would spring things on me for no rhyme or reason. He would renege on bookings I had made, saying that he never agreed to book big stars even though I had raised contracts on them and would try to tell him that an Equity contract once created could not be reneged upon. A good customer of the club, a greengrocer, had seen Tommy's Rolls Royce, a brand new one for every year I had worked for him, parked outside a new shopping precinct in Tottenham. He had a building company and did a lot of work for local councils.

Tommy was pacing across the front of the building when he bumped into the customer, 'Hello Alec.'

'Hello Tom. What you up to?'

'Just pricing up a paint job for the whole of the precinct. How much do you reckon it's worth?'

'How the hell would I know? I'm a grocer.'

Tommy had all the accoutrements of wealth, cars, a farm, stables, everything that money could buy. He thought that the staff were stealing money from him. The point is that artists are always the last to get the money after the owners, agents and managers have had their share. He had threatened to die owing millions. One day he was rushed to hospital with a heart attack. He was not expected to live, but in the words of the song, 'Only the good die young', he survived. Then his wife, who had been a tough, hard-faced employer, became ill and died most unexpectedly. After her funeral her husband began clearing out her wardrobes and dressing rooms and found a fortune in cash stuffed into shoes and boxes and baskets. He had accused his staff of taking the money but it was his wife who had been feathering her nest in case he died.

The club was full to bursting one night and he decided to tell the great pianist Denny Terner we had that he had just destroyed his wife's favourite song, 'Misty', by jazzing it up too much. The pianist, who was the most genned up, cynical, 'been everywhere' musician, had accompanied everyone in the business, quietly closed the grand piano lid and said to the owner, 'If you don't tell me how to play the piano, I won't tell you how to lay bricks.' He picked up his music and left the club, leaving me an hour to find a sight-reading wizard pianist to back Bob Monkhouse.

We had booked a great double act, one of the finest in the business, called Lambert and Ross. They were unknown to the general public but were without doubt one of the funniest double acts in live entertainment. Their reputation was really first class to agents and bookers alike so I was really thrilled to have booked them for a week at the height of the winter season. I had to sell them very hard to the owner of the club because he had never heard of them and thought they would not be a draw. I had to really work hard to get them booked but once I had, I knew I could rely on them to do a great job. Once the public had become aware of them, I would be able to book them right through the year. Their act opened with the straight man coming onto the stage and opening with an operatic song very well sung. Unbeknown to the owner or the crowd, Willy, the funny man, was going around the front tables collecting ashtrays and glasses in a bright red waiter's jacket. At the height of this really dramatic song Willy dropped the tray of glasses and began apologising profusely to the act on stage. The audience and the owner were completely unaware that this was part of the act and the eighteen stone owner rushed full pelt down into the front tables of the club. He grabbed hold of the comic and almost manhandled him up the stairs on the way to being sacked. In true showbusiness spirit, the singer on stage carried on as this melée went on in front of him. Willy pleaded in a broad northern accent with the irate owner to be put down as he was part of the show, and when the audience caught on to what was happening they went wild. Willy shook himself free and the owner then realised what had happened. Lambert and Ross came back to the club as often as I could book them. They were another of the unsung heroes of showbusiness.

The difficulties I had with the owner were incredible. Only once did I ever have to resort to not helping an act get on in the business, I was often asked by managements about the value of acts that I booked at the club. One comedian came to the club having been booked through the owner on a recommendation from some builder friends who had seen him at a golf club cabaret night. I knew the reputation of the comic to be very blue and not the kind of comic we booked at the club except on a real men-only stag nights. Armed with what I knew about this act, I made sure I was at his band call and insisted there was to be no bad language at all and definitely no swearing. He agreed and the evening was set. We always had parties of people for birthdays and anniversaries and there would always be a few children in those parties so we took pride in catering for no-one to be upset or offended by the cabaret. I did my spot and introduced the comic. The first word he said upon reaching the microphone was how *eff-ing delighted* he was to be here and so he went on with a torrent of bad language and comedy. I was peering through the tabs ready to tear him off a strip when the curtains were parted by the owner doing an impression of a bull elephant in musk. He was ranting and raving about me booking this terrible excuse for an entertainer and some of the customers had already complained. As he took his first breath in what seemed like minutes, I interrupted him to say it wasn't me who booked him but the owner himself and that in fact, upon his friends' recommendation, he had been booked twice. The comic finished his act and I barged into his dressing room to give him a serious piece of my mind. As I started my tirade, I failed to notice that the owner was also in the room. He interrupted me by siding with the comic saying that he was obviously unaware of the club's policy on the kind of material we expected from our acts. I stood deflated with my mouth open and said to what looked like two beached whales that weighed thirty-five stone between them that this must be what stupidity looked like in stereo.

I was fuming. I got my revenge though only a week later when I received a phone call from Des O'Connor asking me for my opinion of the said comedian for an appearance on his prime-time chat show. I was able to say that I would not touch him with a bargepole. After the terrible experience Des had with Stan Boardman and his Fokkers, he was always wary. One of the early sayings I learned when I first became aware of how tenuous a life in showbusiness was, 'Be careful what you are prepared to do to get on, because you may meet the same people going up as you do coming down.' If you think of it, you may wonder why some acts who deserved to be famous were not and some acts that were famous seemed to disappear from sight. Much of that stems from not the quality of the act but the politics of their actions and relationships with managements and agencies.

I have come across all kinds of characters in my forty-five years in the biz but Tommy Unwin, the owner of The Starlight, was a law unto himself. He put up houses without building permission. On one house he had a false floor and after the surveyor had inspected the property, he rolled back the carpet to reveal some missing concrete lintels and a staircase down to a huge underground swimming pool and games room. When he died, far from dying a rich man, he lived up to his promise of owing a fortune.

31. Showbiz Changes Direction

The club was really struggling after the owner died. It was taken over by some Greek estate agents who knew even less than the previous owner. The top acts were dying off and people's tastes were changing. We were doing less cabaret and, for the first time in over twenty years, we had to employ bouncers. The whole atmosphere of the club had changed. The nights we did cabaret were getting more and more aggressive; audiences seemed to expect vulgarity and crudeness as it was being pumped out on TV sets in their own frontrooms. Comics seemed to have applied the same maxim that Brits abroad use: instead of learning the language, shout as loud as you can and you will get the audience to *efffing* understand what you are on about, even if they are foreign. They helped to abolish the status quo, of good taste, subtlety and nuance, and they helped to bring down the establishment and promote yoof culture and some went on to make millions and become part of the showbusiness aristocracy.

Showbusiness as I knew it died for me New Year's Eve 1999. I did my last show ever although I didn't know it would be my last at the time. New Year's Eve at the club was a huge eight-hour marathon for me. It started at 7 p.m. and ended at 3 a.m. We served a six-course meal, there was dancing and a top class cabaret, and then more dancing to bring in the new year. A full breakfast of eggs, bacon, sausage, tomatoes, fried bread, the lot, was served at 1.30 a.m., and we finished the evening off by taking a trip down memory lane with old-time songs. New Year's Eve had always been the best show of very many difficult years but this year it was spoiled by something that had never happened in over twenty years: a huge fight broke out. When I left the club at four that morning, I said goodbye to it for the last time. The renowned football club was driven into bancruptcy and sold off and the nightclub closed to become a housing estate. I left knowing that I had seen the best of showbusiness and wondering what I would do next.

A Short Modelling Career

As well as all the other things I was involved in, I even got around to doing some modelling. I have to say I found it very unrewarding. A good commercial was worth a lot of money but all the call-ups to London and the recalls and the rejection slips were so demoralising. You spent a lot of time and money only to be rejected. I did manage to get the voiceover for one of the very early Yellow Pages adverts. That was my voice saying, 'Let your fingers do the walking,' and they used my finger too. Fame at last! I was even on the shortlist for the Milk Tray advert where the guy jumps off cliffs and everything, 'And all because the lady Loves Milk Tray.' I had to go to a casting in St. Martin's Lane, London. I knew that I was not a natural model, I just looked half decent and was quite athletic. I scaled a flight of stairs and rang the bell.

I walked into a room full of the greatest looking men I had ever seen. They were all over six foot tall, square-jawed, tanned Adonises. I felt positively scruffy and inept in a room full of male perfection. They all seemed to know each other and were sharing stories of commercials they had just been on in Jamaica, South Africa and America. I ducked down behind my newspaper and hid until I was called. They were chatting away when the doorbell rang. I wasn't going to open it so I carried on reading the paper. The bell rang again and nobody moved – they were so wrapped up in their stories. The bell rang again and the presser just leant on it until a six foot two hero got gracefully up and strode, à la John Wayne, towards the door. He opened it with a flourish and standing there was another six foot two Victor Mature lookalike. For those too young to remember, Victor Mature was a Hollywood filmstar who played Samson in *Samson and Delilah*. The guy had an immaculate camel-hair coat draped over his broad shoulders. I cringed at the prospect of being considered in the same class as these guys and slunk down in my seat. Victor stood in the doorway, arms akimbo, drew a deep breath and said in the highest camp voice, 'What's up girls? Have we all got broken femurs, or can't you stand the competition?' I was screaming inside by now. It seemed that nearly everyone in the room was gay except me.

Three things for a straight man not to say in a gay bar anywhere: 'Blow me, it's hot in here.' 'I'll toss you for the next round' and 'Can I push your stool in for you?' The gay performers I worked with in all areas of the entertainment industry were without doubt the funniest people I have ever met.

A life full of colourful characters

My whole professional life has been spent with the most colourful characters. Everyone seemed to be living on the edge of the law and everything seemed to be easy come, easy go. I have been blessed to be able to experience the joy and laughter of living on the edge but I also saw the pain and aggravation of having to pay the price of getting caught. I had one friend, a typical nightclub friend and a serious heavyweight villain. Immaculately dressed in the George Raft style and a man of very few words. You would not know if you had upset him but if you had, the retribution would be very painful and very bad. He surprised me one evening by stringing together a whole sentence rather than the usual monsyllabes he usually imparted with a smile and a nod.

Gesticulating with choreographed hand movements he said, 'J.J., it's all gone south.'

'What's that, John?' I asked.

'Villainy,' he said.

'Why?'

''Cos no-one knows who the baddies are anymore. All these young kids are tooled up and everybody is getting done, young and old, even good people.'

In the old days all we had to fight were other villains or West

Central Police, who were bigger villains than we were.

Dennis and Henry kept in touch. I would go to The Windsor Theatre, or a Ray Clooney production that Henry was appearing in, usually a farce like *Run For Your Life With Your Trousers Down*. Dennis finally got employed directing Freddie Starr's new series. Then he was invited to go to Spain to direct the Spanish equivalent of The Benny Hill Show and then went to Ireland to do a whole series of comedy programmes.

One of the saddest things I ever experienced was when I was asked to go back to Thames at Teddington by some in-house producers who wanted me to compère a pilot show for a new talent show they had thought of. Although they still rented offices at Thames, it was to be financed by themselves and sold independently. I walked back into Thames TV and, unlike in the past, the carpark was almost empty. I walked through the foyer that was once bustling with all kinds of talented artists and technicians to be greeted by a lone security officer. I walked down a corridor that once rang with laughter past huge photographs of Benny Hill, Des O'Connor, Morecombe and Wise, Tommy Cooper and Jim Davidson, to the sound of my own hollow footsteps. I made my way to the offices that were now empty and bare, then to the producer's office and bemoaned the sadness of the empty shell that was once a joyous bustling hive that produced some of the best TV comedy ever made. Once there were two thousand people employed at Thames and now it was just a shell. The laughter that once rang out through the whole building had now died and with it came back the memories of the wonderful times I had spent here in the past.

Monte Carlo & The Raniers

I took time out to catch up with family and friends. Some good friends had sold their hotel business and gone to retire in Monte Carlo. Because of my experience of building our own house, our friends always called upon us to help them to move. It was so rewarding to catch all the things that people no longer wanted, old antiques and such like, put them in my shed at home and work on them and bring them back to life. We became frequent visitors to Monaco and I ended up getting involved

Jon Jon introduced by Miss Sarah Keable to His Royal Highness Prince Rainier of Monaco

with charity events in the Principality. I met Prince Albert - that would have been a big feather in my cap for my Mum and Dad if they had been alive, bless 'em. I spent a wonderful evening in the company of Prince Rainier's sister Antoinette singing songs from the Stanley Holloway song book, a great love of hers as she had spent

226

many years of the war in Yorkshire. Two very funny insights into the human condition are: that no matter what we aspire to, certain little things stick in our minds that would seem so trivial to an onlooker. Sir Stanley Holloway upon his death bed was asked by his son if there were any great regrets in his life. Even though he had risen from the East End to become Sir Stanley Holloway, he was really miffed that James Hayter had got the voiceover for McVitties Jaffa Cakes and not him. The Poet Laureate Sir John Betjeman upon his death bed when asked the same question said he regretted not having had enough sex.

32. **Health is Everything**

So here I was, sixty years young, still fit - playing badminton and squash and swimming. Life was good and I had no plans to ever retire. But one day the world fell on my head and it compressed my internal organs to the point of them acquiring a mind of their own and henceforth would say when, where and how often they would empty themselves with no recourse to head office, Jon Jon. Unaware of the sudden collapse of the front-loading and rear-loading waste product recycling mechanisms, J.J. thought that this was just the result of a sixty year journey with the hardships of life. My personal survival over the years since I was thrown to the dogs as a war baby, struggling with very little subsistance in times of national deprivation, surviving bombing from a continental foe only to emerge into a free world, a venture into a state education with an intellect that seemed to surpass its menial surroundings. My future had looked grim, thrust into a world of work at fifteen years of age with no qualifications. With only J.J. to fall back on, I had enough determination to not only survive but to bloody-well achieve some status in life.

Showbiz... the jungle... rejection.. I was alone again . Then one day a stroke of good fortune, followed by a wonderful wife, a mortgage, three children, school fees, repairing cars for school runs, mending washing machines, building a house, digging, plumbing and all the time to try to be a caring person.

Waterworks Breakdown

It must be a slow progress of deterioration that gets you to the point where all your systems begin to break down. In my case it was at the big six-o when the waterworks decided to take on a mind of their own and I could not go fifteen minutes or three miles from the house. I had a burning pain, constant trips to the doctors, an internal examination to explore in a place where no man had been before! A large camera was inserted (this is an authentic medical territory we have entered, not some airing of a kinky e-mail) into the end of Jon Jon's penis. This was followed by a mechanical device similar to an apparatus you use at a funfair, trying to grab a useless little bear or a packet of sweets that it would be easier to buy. The incredible pain even with a local anesthetic was 'Aye Carrumbah!' Being stoic and of hardy stock, I steeled myself, eyes watering, lips biting, and trying to restrain myself from grabbing the Eastern ethnic white-coated butcher of Baghadad doctor I believed him when he said this sample of my severed bladder was on its way to the laboratory. After some considerable lapse of time, as the doctors tried to cure the infection that the procedure had caused in the said organ (sadly underused in these latter years), the results after the infection cleared up were quite pleasing, in as much as there was some untoward blemish on the wall of J.J.'s bladder. But it was not the Big C. It was in fact Interstitial Cystitis, an equally fearful foe, little known to the medical profession. Meanwhile, back at the ranch and alone again, I can still not go far from a toilet and the problem seems to be getting worse. My urologist is puzzled and suggests a trip into a relative of the 'front box', the 'back box'. So another doctor a relative of the front box operator, another eastern ethnic white-coated potentae with white rubber gloves, rolls me on my side, and he seems intent on getting his own back for my part in England's occupation of India. He proceeds to go where no man has ever been before, or will go again, first delving into my back box, testing the size of my prostate with a rubber-coated finger. He seems satisfied with this examination and, with my eyes severely watering and thinking that was the end of it, I open my eyes to see him advancing towards me with a large camera on a bendy stick. It dawns on me that although I have been in front of many different cameras, how many of my showbiz friends had been photographed from the inside out! I satisfied myself that at least I would be the member of a very exclusive club. But there would be no residuals this time! The results were rewarding in as much as I did not pick up an infection this time and the *grim reaper* was not evident in my 'back box', just a severe case of Diverticulitis – another incurable condition!

Exploring Alternative Medicine

So, armed with the proof of the pukka medical profession, not being able to treat these conditions, I am proffered some sound advice 'to explore alternative medicine' and am given the address of a kinestheologist in the wilds of East Grinstead. For me this was a humungous trip across country around the always snarled-up M25. On a good day, with a following wind, this trip that would take at least and hour and a half. Or, in my case, six pisses and two possible craps away.

So I set off on a journey that I had been unable to even contemplate for six months, suitably attired in a track suit with bottoms for a quick release of body fluids. I set off alone. I reached my journey's end in excruciating pain and knocked feebly on the door. A small wizened kinesthetic practitioner greeted me and I gently brushed her aside in search of the toilet. The relief was bigger than the historical legendary 'Relief of Mafeking'.

Having relieved myself, I proceeded to divulge my journey through sleepless nights and unimaginable pain, six visits per night to the toilet, by now an almost broken man. As she listened intently, she made me feel that she was truly concerned. But, it was for financial gain, of course, and the first consultation extracted a bill of £175. The consultation lasted for two hours and I left with a supply of vitamin and homeopathic remedies and information about my 50% dehydration and the need for me to drink at least three litres of water a day.

Now considering that I have been visiting the front box toilet between fifteen and twenty times a day, this seemed a somewhat frightening prospect. My homeopathic helper allayed my fears by saying that I had been exhausting my fluid content from a depleted reservoir and that this would aid all my systems to return to the status quo. Not having to go to the front box toilet so often and because of a deformation of my intestinal wall that traps waste product in the diverticular folds that become infected, then the herbal medicaments will induce a natural expulsion of the waste products. So, I was armed with what seemed to be a natural remedy without the side-effects that prescribed medicine had caused me. Having experienced a psychotic breakdown for ten days when a course of morphine-based patches mixed with another prescribed drug and caused me to go nutty, I swore that no matter how painful my conditions were, I would not rely on prescribed painkillers again.

Gen up as much as you can on your own predicaments, learn how to live with the fear of it. If it doesn't kill you, it is only pain that you fear. We are all alone, naturally, so deal with it and stay alive. I have found that light-heartedness and laughter are the staple food of inner power. Add to this lots of water, fresh air, good food and excercise to promote a long a happy life.

Homeopathy was just one of the adventures in dealing with my conditions. I have had four cystoscopies, a C.T. scan, two M.R.I. scans, an ultrasound, two colonoscopies and any number of enemas. Frank Carson tells a joke of when he went into hospital for exploratory tests. He said he was given an enema at 10 a.m., an enema at 12 noon and an enema at 2 p.m. He said, 'I fell asleep exhausted and was awakened by another nurse who I asked, "Are you a friend or an enema?".'

Tests for some eminent physcians brought forth no more than a shrug of their shoulders in front of me. For a couple of years I became morose and dejected, not able to get any respite from these illnesses at all. I became the proverbial pain in the arse to my family and friends and it is only now that I have been able to cheer myself up by looking back on a most fortunate life.

33. Over the Hill

In praise of the fading Benny Hill Muskateers

I am one of the only Benny Hill Muskateers still alive. On 28th January 2006, I went along with some of the most noted actors still alive, to the funeral of Henry Marris McGee. Henry was the single most kind, talented professional person I ever met. Quiet, studious and with a wicked sense of humour. I always sent Christmas cards to him and phoned from time to time. I had not had a reply for some time and I found it hard to get in touch with him as he never had a telephone, only an answerphone. You would leave a message and he would get back to you. But I happened to read in a paper that he had been unwell and I tried to track him down. Secret as ever, he had gone into a theatrical nursing home for a while and I managed to find out which one after many a wild goose chase. The lovely Anna Dawson, who was Benny's favourite lady stooge and who is married to the lovely-voiced John Boulter of The Black and White Minstrel Show fame, phoned me to say she had found out that Henry was in a private nursing home in Putney and we made arrangements to go to visit him. We were met by the saddest sight, our Henry who was famous for his ability to memorise difficult scripts at what seemed like a glance, living in a beautiful nursing home but struck down so cruelly, with *Senile Dementia.* We saw him briefly for it seemed to unerve him because he just did not know who we were, even though I had spent sixteen years of my life with this wonderful man!

Anna and I almost shed a tear at his terrible condition, but Anna made the case for us to be the only ones to be sorry because Henry was totally unaware of his condition. Henry died and was laid to rest with all the gentle pomp and gravitas that he would have loved, with beautiful words spoken by Sir Donald Sinden.

Dennis Kirkland- the great comedy director

I then had a call from the Executive Producer of The Benny Hill Show, Nigel Cooke. Nigel was equally one of the Muskateers. A Public Schoolboy, Times crossword buff. Always able to add a pertinent sensible view in a maelstrom of uneducated actors pissed up communications. He asked me if I had heard how ill Dennis Kirkland was. He had been taken into hospital and the treatment they had been giving him for one condition had gone wrong and he was fighting for his life as only Dennis could. I telephoned his beautiful wife Mary and she told me a story of absolute horror. Dennis had been taken into hospital for one condition but the diagnosis and the treatment had been incorrect and Dennis was now on a life support machine. Dennis was a tenacious little Geordie, fiercely proud of his roots. In happier times we would challenge each other on the great North-vs-South divide. The problem was, I was much taller than he was and he spent a great deal of time cutting me down to size. He was a walking encyclopedia of comedy. He could have been a comic himself but he loved the process of getting the very best out of the comic he was working with and understanding all their fears and foibles. Comedians as a rule are insecure and loners, the pressure of making

235

people laugh is incredibly nerve-racking. There seem to be very few people they can trust to get the gag off the page and into life. To have someone you can trust implicitly to get your work across is a huge benefit to them.

I can truly say that I never heard Dennis denigrate any artists. He was aware of the difficulty of producing a constantly rewarding programme when critics were poised to pillory comics in their pursuit of making people smile. Benny was flogged incessantly as a dirty old man, even though it was very far from the truth. You only had to ask the ladies who appeared on the show. In fact when the programme was resold to America they asked for the costumes to be even briefer on the dancer but Benny said no. After each critical beating that Ben took it was Dennis who made him smile and pitched him back into the fray. I only ever saw Dennis down once in all the time we worked together. We had been on a really difficult shoot, the weather was atrocious and we were really behind schedule. The budget was a real source of contention with the management, Benny was not feeling too well and things were tough. We went to rushes after a hard day in the wind, rain and snow. We were shooting a scene in swimming costumes, supposedly in the summer, but the snowflakes were showing up on camera. Dennis had *little in the can* [very little film shot] that day and was very disconsolate. And try as I may to cheer him up, it was to no avail. We had a few drinks in The Anglers and we went home.

I phoned him at home later in the evening and I said, 'Excuse me, is this my director, *the* Dennis Kirkland speaking?'

He said tersely, 'Yes. What do you want, Keefe?'

I said 'It is not about me but about thee that I am ringing. Is it true that I am a six foot actor?'

'Yes,' he said, 'what do you want?'

'Bear with me, O great one,' I said. 'And is it true that you are a five foot four Geordie?'

'Five foot six,' he said.

'Do you know or care how difficult it is for a six foot Cockney to have to look up to a five foot four Geordie?'

'Just what are you getting at?' he snapped.

I said, 'If you did understand, then you would understand how difficult it was for me to physically and mentally look up to my director, the master of the ship we sail, in the endeavour of bringing mirth to a sombre nation. It is in your hands alone to be virile and potent and masterful, there are so many people relying on you to get us through, just you, O great one.' I flattered and bolstered him to the point of him almost firing me, for having seen what no other human at Thames TV had ever seen, Dennis Kirkland being vulnerable.

He took a deep breath and said, 'Keefe, if this conversation gets out, you are a dead man.'

I knew I had done my job of bolstering my director up to his usual solid confidence. Next day I arrived at the studio greeted Den and he told me to go put on a dress some high heels and an old wig. I knew I had succeeded as the rest of the cast were dressed for a whole day's shooting as Spanish toreadors. The incident was never spoken of again, I just knew he loved me for the great friends we were.

The Myth of Showbiz Glamour

It is so strange people's concept of the glamour showbiz is supposed to provide. Outside of the biz, it all looks so easy. The truth is fame and fortune falls on just a few and it seems that as a nation we build people up just to knock them down. The rest of the population of grafting performers get the crumbs but are forever working hard to get to the top of the ladder. The beautiful girls on Benny's show were talented and pretty. The mainstay was Sue Upton who Ben cherished, the beautiful Louise English and Lorraine Doyle. He used these ladies constantly. The Hill's Angels were changed for each series. They had to be great dancers and able to act in some of the sketches. They were so unlike what the public may have perceived them to be. They were beautiful and talented but many of them lacked the desire to get any further than what they were involved in at any one time. Most of them were mainly involved with boyfriends who were ordinary guys like plumbers, car dealers, just genuine jack-the-lads. On location they would huddle around the gas heaters in their caravans and it would take all kinds of threats to get them onto the freezing cold set dressed in swimming costumes in the middle of winter. I soon sussed out that if they were a long time coming, Den would have to set up some other shots, so I would always be by the side of the camera in case he needed anyone to fill out a scene. Henry was always nearby and as soon as Dennis asked for some artists to fill out a scene Henry and I would hotfoot it to wardrobe to get dressed in whatever uniform the scene needed.

One day Ben was shooting some scenes with his kids. They were in fact the children of the choreographers, Libby Roberts, Sue Upton and Dennis Kirkland. Ben treated the children like the family he never had and spoiled them rotten, but they were the children of pros so they knew what was expected of them. There was a scene in Ben's garden, Ben was messing about with the kids close up to the camera, Dennis asked for someone to dress the back of the shot, an old gardener or something. I rushed off to wardrobe and got dressed as an old gardener and went quickly into make up to be heavily disguised. Dennis was getting wised up to Henry and I being in most shots, in the background, over to the side in a car any where that he needed someone to walk through a shot. We went back to the studios to watch the day's rushes and Den was as pleased as punch with Ben and the kids' performance.

Then he said to Angie Carter. 'Who the hell is the old guy taking a lifetime sweeping leaves in the background? He's in every frame I can cut the sketch into.'

Angie looked at the cast notes and said, 'That's Jon Jon.'

Dennis punched me and said, 'You bastard. You got yourself a pension in just that one sketch.'

In unison we both sang 'residuals.'

Dennis never let it lie. He had the greatest way of comically getting his own back on me. Next day was spent in the interminable dress, high heels and wig. Henry and Toddy commiserated with me but just told me to think of the residuals dear boy.

Dennis Kirkland Dies

Dennis died and was buried on 1st March 2006. There were over five hundred people at his funeral. He had applied as a boy to be a property master trainee when he worked at Tyne Tees Television as a seventeen year old. At his interview he was told that he would never achieve such a high ambition. Like the true Geordie terrier he was, he went on to be one of the top comedy directors in all of British entertainment!

The attendance at his funeral was proof of the love people had for this dynamic bundle of fun. His wife, Mary, and his beautiful daughter, Jo, asked me to pay tribute to my great friend. I collected all the stories of a professional life spent with him. I leaned heavily on his fellow Muskateers, myself, Henry, Toddy and Jackie and our love and joy of having him as a friend and thanking him for our residuals. Chas and Dave sang his favourite song of theirs, 'There Ain't No Pleasing You'. Stories followed which showed the two completely different aspects of his life. The one spent propped up at his local pub, laughing and gagging about the pressure of being a comic genius and the other as a family man and professional. In true style his coffin was carried from the church to the thumping sounds of Jerry Lee Lewis singing 'Great Balls Of Fire'.

Back at the reception the mood was full of laughter and noise everyone recalling their own personal stories of this great guy. Mary thanked me for the speech I made, for setting exactly the right tone for people to be able to relax and smile and tell funny stories about Den. Den would have wanted his passing to be a joyous occasion and Mary said I set the atmosphere for all on this very sad day.

Nigel Cooke and I left the church, looked at each other and said, 'Ah well, who's next? Me or thee?'

Pursue Your Dreams and Never Give Up

I wrote this story because my best friend, James Hall, insisted that I had some thing worthwhile to say. It's a story of the behind-the-scenes of a showbiz no longer alive. His thoughts are 'that everybody has the desire to do something great, many have the determination, but very few of us have the discipline to just do it'. So I did it.

So here is the story which I began, wondering why I could never make the big time and top of the bill, but ends with me thinking how well I have done. Not a case of always the bridesmaid never the bride, but having achieved a position in posterity afforded to very few in my business. If we are all seeking immortality then, whenever Charlie Chaplin, Buster Keaton, Laurel and Hardy, W.C.Fields and now Benny Hill are played, as part of Benny's crew, I will be locked on celluloid as part of a group of performers and friends who tried nothing more than to bring some joy into this crazy world we live in. I will die a happy man knowing how much I have been cared for by

241

my darling family and my friends.

I want to encourage everybody to pursue their dream and **never give up.** All the pros I met were driven by the same need, especially the comedians, because when your gags work, it's the greatest feeling in the world, but when they don't, you're alone again naturally. So just press on, live in the moment and just get as much joy from this day as possible.

'That's all Folks'

34. The last piece of the Jigsaw.

Just as I came to the end of this story a fantastic thing happened and made me add this wonderful experience.

For my seventieth birthday my son and daughters and my cousin Terry hatched a plot to give me a surprise present to prove or disprove the never ending stories of hard ship and deprivation I had bombarded them with since they were born, and especially now I had joined the grumpy old men's club.

Once-and-for-all they wanted to put to rest stories of the trials and tribulations that I had been through. So on the seventh of March 2009 at 9am a coach turned up at my house followed by my cousin, his wife Bridget and his four middle-aged children and with the addition of some boy and girl friends we were now sixteen in number. A breakfast of bacon butties and tea was quickly dispatched and a noisy excited group boarded the coach.

We headed down the M25 - first stop Dagenham. The conversation on the coach was full of comical put downs about my cousin and I being like the two old guys on The Muppets. We said we would show them how we had toughened it out and if it wasn't for us they wouldn't be here. My cousin had researched part of the family tree and filled me in with some of the childhood memories of lost aunts and uncles and where they had lived in London. I was given a large photograph showing a grey-haired moustachioed gentleman on the stairs, suited and booted. My cousin asked me if I knew who it was, I thought I had got it in a boot sale. He said it was my great great-granddad and the photo underneath it was my heroic uncle Johnny and for the first time in over sixty years I was able to put faces to two people I had heard many stories about when I was a child. This was just one of the many things that was going to be revealed on this incredible day.

We reached Dagenham and went to the house we had been given after being 'bombed out' in Bethnal Green. We alighted from the coach and walked into the banjo where I had a photograph taken outside my old house with my arm around my sons shoulder to replicate a photograph I had taken with my brother in 1949.

I remembered all the names of the twelve families that had lived in the banjo and curtains were now being pulled back to see this motley crew, wondering what we were doing there.

The next stop was Valance Park where the children were waiting to see the famous swimming pool we had spoken so much about. However it was now gone. We had to settle for real football pitches manned now by some football coach who was impressed when we told him we had played in this park with just clothes for goalposts and that the park had spawned players of great fame like Jimmy Greaves Terry Venebles, Ken Brown, Les Allen and many more.

Next stop was my first primary school and St Josephs Church, followed by Rush Green cemetery where my father, my mother, my Aunt Connie and my incredible Grandma were buried. The family were most impressed with the cultivated well-kept gravestones and said they had never seen so many fresh cut flowers in a graveyard. We paid our respects and cried tears of sorrow and joy.

We all boarded the coach and headed for the East-end of London while my cousin and I told them they had never had it so good as our stoic and steadfast upbringings lacked all the supposed luxuries like bananas and oranges that their generation take for granted. A chorus of boos and cheers greeted our meanderings. The coach went through Stratford, Whitechapel, and Mile End. First stop was for lunch at The Apprentice Restaurant. My cousin told us that the reason for eating here was that it was formerly St Monica's Roman Catholic School where my mother, aunt Nellie and aunt Connie went to school. The school was then in one of the poorest parts of London which has now become one of the most salubrious places to live, particularly Hoxton Square. The City of London and Sir Alan Sugar have turned the school into The Apprentice Restaurant to teach under privileged young people a trade in the catering business. It is next to the rejuvenated St Monica's church where my mother and her two sisters were baptised and married and where my cousin and I were baptised.

I considered how bitter I have felt that my grandfather had gone off to fight for King and Country and had died on the Somme at 35, the oldest man in his regiment compelled by goodness-knows-what national pride,to leave his wife and three little girls.,My mother was only two months old when he was killed. My grandma came from a family of eight and my cousins father came from a family of thirteen and what they had to do to survive was unimaginable.

Just around the corner from the Apprentice Restaurant, my family were fed from a soup kitchen supplied by a New Zealand charitable organisation. There were no social security or pensions or any government hand-outs so everyone was left to their own resources to care for themselves. I have to research how my grandma did it and I am incensed at the total lack of care that was shown to them and their whole generation. So they were sent off as cannon fodder to save the free world and history has shown us what a farce that turned out to be. I experienced some of what they went through as I was born in 1939. Mr Neville Chamberlain' said 'Peace in our time' as we went off to save the free world once again. What a load of old cobblers that has turned out to be as the frontiers of our country have been thrown open and the whole world comes looking for hand-outs.

I hope you can see how deeply I felt as I immersed myself in part of my family's history surrounded by all the people who had benefited by our parents and grand-parents sacrifices. They completely understood why my cousin and I had banged on the way we have all of their lives and they were very moved.

Back on the coach again around to Colombia Row where we had been bombed out to Hassard Street where we had lived after staying on Bethnal Green underground station for a while. We walked the streets animated and excited and were applauded by our children as genuine portrayers of unembellished true stories. .

Back on the coach again we headed down the M4 motorway excited, moved and fulfilled and we all began to sing as we had become closer than we ever thought possible, having shared this fantastic experience together.

Jon Jon [with glasses] surrounded by his family and partners celebrating his 70th after reliving the past

We arrived home and had a great party, with the knowledge that our children would now pass on what they had seen for themselves to their own children and maybe even take the same journey to let them know who they really were.

My life is now fulfilled as I know who I am and where I came from and why I think the way I do.

I take pride in this and do not feel that I need any further acclimation or fame and hope you will forgive my honesty, as I am not attempting to be smug - just glowingly content with my lot .

Jon Jon Keefe [AKA Brian Kearney]

September 2009